LIGHT, HAPPINESS AND PEACE

Visit our web site at
www.albahouse.org
(for orders www.alba-house.com)
or call 1-800-343-2522 (ALBA)
and request current catalog

Light, Happiness and Peace

Journeying Through Traditional Catholic Spirituality

FR. JOHN J. PASQUINI

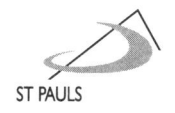

ST PAULS

Alba
House

Library of Congress Cataloging-in-Publication Data

Pasquini, John J.
  Light, happiness and peace: journeying through traditional Catholic Spirituality / John J. Pasquini.
    p. cm.
  Includes bibliographical references.
    ISBN 0-8189-0957-9
  1. Spiritual life—Catholic Church. I. Title

    BX2350.3.P37 2004
    248.4'82—dc21
                                2003012036

Produced and designed in the United States of America by the Fathers and Brothers of the Society of St. Paul, 2187 Victory Boulevard, Staten Island, New York 10314-6683, as part of their communications apostolate.

ISBN: 0-8189-0957-9

© Copyright 2004 by the Society of St. Paul

Printing Information:

Current Printing - first digit   1   2   3   4   5   6   7   8   9   10

Year of Current Printing - first year shown

2004   2005   2006   2007   2008   2009   2010   2011   2012   2013

*Dedicated to
my precious mother, Florence,
and in memory of my beloved father, Renato*

Table of Contents

Preface ix

Introduction xi

Chapter 1: The Awakening 1

Chapter 2: Foundational Points 7

Chapter 3: The Purgative Stage
The Age of the Superficial 55

Chapter 4: The First Dark Night
The Active Purification of the Senses 83

Chapter 5: The Second Part of the First Dark Night
The Passive Purification of the Senses 89

Chapter 6: The Illuminative Stage
A Time of Enlightenment 99

Chapter 7: The Second Dark Night
The Passive Purification of the Spirit
(or Passive Purification of the Spiritual Soul) 133

Chapter 8: The Unitive Stage
A Taste of Heaven 139

Appendix: Explaining Salvation and Mysticism
in People of Other Faiths 159

Preface

There are two realities we deal with every day of our lives. On the one hand we desire a life of happiness, peace and contentment, and on the other hand we recognize that life comes with suffering. How do we reconcile these two realities?

As Christians we believe that Christ reconciles these two realities; that in Christ, the Reconciler, we can have a taste of happiness, a taste of peace and contentment, even amidst a life that inevitably and unavoidably comes with suffering, with trials and tribulations.

Holiness is a voyage toward light, happiness and peace. It is a journey toward "wholeness" and toward authentic "humanness."

In a world that thirsts and aches for meaning and purpose, the spiritual life provides the means for attaining this purpose and meaning.

Light, Happiness and Peace: Journeying Through Traditional Catholic Spirituality summarizes and explains the best of Catholic prayer and spiritual development. It is a blueprint in which day-to-day Catholics can find fulfillment.

Abbreviations

AAS	*Acta Apostolicae Sedis*
Ascent	*The Ascent of Mount Carmel* (St. John of the Cross)
CCC	*Catechism of the Catholic Church*
Dark Night	*The Dark Night of the Soul* (St. John of the Cross)
DS	Denzinger-Schönmetzer, *Enchiridion Symbolorum*
GILH	General Introduction to the Liturgy of the Hours
GS	*Gaudium et Spes* (Vatican II, Pastoral Constitution on the Church in the Modern World)
Interior Castle	*The Interior Castle* (St. Teresa of Avila)
LG	*Lumen Gentium* (Vatican II, Dogmatic Constitution on the Church)
Life	*The Book of Her Life* (St. Teresa of Avila)
Living Flame	*The Living Flame of Love* (St. John of the Cross)
PG	*Patrologia Graeca*
PL	*Patrologia Latina*
Spiritual Canticle	*The Spiritual Canticle* (St. John of the Cross)
ST	*Summa Theologiae* (St. Thomas Aquinas)
Treatise	*Treatise on the Love of God* (St. Francis de Sales)
Way	*The Way of Perfection* (St. Teresa of Avila)

Introduction

How many times have we become delayed in our travels because of a lack of direction? How many times have we pondered that if we only had a map we would find the way safely and more quickly? Whenever embarking on a long and arduous journey, we always need to have a map at hand to guide us through to our destination effectively and securely.

What can be said of our "worldly" travels can be said of our spiritual journey. Getting to the destination is a matter of responding to grace, but this response to grace can be made much more effective and safe if we have a general idea of where we are going. And so just as there is a map for a "worldly" trip, there is also a map for the spiritual journey, a map that has been written through years of experience with grace.

While it is true that there are no two journeys completely alike in the spiritual life, there is a general pattern that can be traced. It is this pattern we will explore in this book.

The first stage of the spiritual life involves the purgative stage, a stage of purification. It is followed by the illuminative stage, a stage of great enlightenment and integration. The third and final stage is the unitive stage. This is the stage of the mystics. It is the stage where one's will and God's will are united to such an extent that one may say, without much reservation, that every action performed is an action of God.

What a gift! What a journey! Let us read about this journey, but more importantly, let us seek to respond to grace and live out this journey, the ultimate journey to light, happiness and peace.

Biblical Abbreviations

OLD TESTAMENT

Genesis	Gn	Nehemiah	Ne	Baruch	Ba
Exodus	Ex	Tobit	Tb	Ezekiel	Ezk
Leviticus	Lv	Judith	Jdt	Daniel	Dn
Numbers	Nb	Esther	Est	Hosea	Ho
Deuteronomy	Dt	1 Maccabees	1 M	Joel	Jl
Joshua	Jos	2 Maccabees	2 M	Amos	Am
Judges	Jg	Job	Jb	Obadiah	Ob
Ruth	Rt	Psalms	Ps	Jonah	Jon
1 Samuel	1 S	Proverbs	Pr	Micah	Mi
2 Samuel	2 S	Ecclesiastes	Ec	Nahum	Na
1 Kings	1 K	Song of Songs	Sg	Habakkuk	Hab
2 Kings	2 K	Wisdom	Ws	Zephaniah	Zp
1 Chronicles	1 Ch	Sirach	Si	Haggai	Hg
2 Chronicles	2 Ch	Isaiah	Is	Malachi	Ml
Ezra	Ezr	Jeremiah	Jr	Zechariah	Zc
		Lamentations	Lm		

NEW TESTAMENT

Matthew	Mt	Ephesians	Eph	Hebrews	Heb
Mark	Mk	Philippians	Ph	James	Jm
Luke	Lk	Colossians	Col	1 Peter	1 P
John	Jn	1 Thessalonians	1 Th	2 Peter	2 P
Acts	Ac	2 Thessalonians	2 Th	1 John	1 Jn
Romans	Rm	1 Timothy	1 Tm	2 John	2 Jn
1 Corinthians	1 Cor	2 Timothy	2 Tm	3 John	3 Jn
2 Corinthians	2 Cor	Titus	Tt	Jude	Jude
Galatians	Gal	Philemon	Phm	Revelation	Rv

The Awakening

> People are hungry for God. People are hungry for love. Are you aware of that? Do you know that? Do you see that? Do you have eyes to see? Quite often we look but we don't see. We are all passing through this world. We need to open our eyes and see.[1]
> *Mother Teresa*

When we open our eyes to the reality of God, then we can be said to have been awakened. There is a point in our life where we are faced with the reality that there is something which is beyond the self, something which transcends the limits of our being. This moment is a moment of choice. Do we seek to explore and enter into this mystery of that which is beyond the limits of the self or do we repress the experience? The choice made is the choice that will help govern our life.

What "voice" attracts someone to God?

We are awakened and moved to follow the ways of grace by being enlightened to the presence of God. Traditionally, people have been attracted to God in the following ways:

---

[1] Mother Teresa, *One Heart Full of Love* (Ann Arbor: Servant Publications, 1984), 11.

Meaning and Purpose

People are often awakened or attracted to God because God gives them a sense of meaning and purpose in life (cf. Dt 6:24-25). We recognize that we must be more than some complex organism that is born, lives, struggles, and dies in emptiness. Life in many ways would be a farce if that were so. Life would be inevitably on the edge of disintegration. No, there must be more to life than mere existence, than mere survival.

Life needs purpose and meaning, a purpose and meaning that transcends the here and now.

God provides this purpose and meaning. He provides each person with a priestly, kingly, and prophetic life. We are called to be priestly by bringing Christ's healing and reconciling presence to those in need; likewise, we are called to be open to receiving that same reconciling and healing presence brought by others in the name of Christ for our own self. We are called to a kingly life by recognizing our dignity as a human being and by recognizing the dignity of all life from conception to natural death. This calling also entails a vocation of seeking justice for all. We are called to the prophetic life by standing up for the truth, no matter what the cost. The martyrs exemplified this aspect in extraordinary ways. Seeking God, living in God, and carrying out his mission of the *good news* as well as in preparing the way for the Lord are all aspects that provide meaning and purpose to life.

A life with purpose and meaning is a happy life. Despair is always associated to some degree with the loss of meaning and purpose.

Truth

Many are attracted to God because God is Truth (1 Jn 4:6, 24; 1 Tm 3:5). Such people seek truth in life, no matter where they may find it. Their life is a quest for this truth. Such people find great comfort in God for he is truth itself. Hence, life becomes for such individuals a delving into the mysteries of God, which consumes the entirety of their lives and gives them the ultimate in joy. St. Thomas Aquinas in many ways exemplified the reality of this search for truth as did the great philosophers St. Edith Stein and Jacques Maritain.

Good

Some people find God by seeing the good around them. Malcolm Muggeridge, a world-renowned reporter for the BBC, was such a person in many respects. It was in seeing the good that was in the heart of Mother Teresa of Calcutta that he was able to find Christ. In Mother Teresa he saw Jesus Christ, and his life would never be the same again. Likewise, it was in the goodness of St. Francis of Assisi that the poor and disenfranchised would come back to the Church, even amidst their struggles. It was in seeing the good in St. Joan of Arc that a whole nation fought for its independence and dignity. God is good, and those who have found authentic goodness have found God (cf. Rm 12:2).

Beautiful

Many are attracted to God because they see in the beauty of creation the handprint of God. St. Augustine, St. Bonaventure, and St. Francis can be said to exemplify this reality. For them all of creation echoed the beauty and providence of God. To find authentic beauty is to find the source of all beauty, God (cf. Ws 13:3).

The Four Ways

While it is true that most people will find an affinity for one of the above ways or "voices of God," all the above ways or "voices" should be a part of a person's attraction to God. An individual should make it his or her constant prayer to grow in the ways that he or she may perceive, in grace, to be an area of growth.

The spiritual life is about balance and moderation. One's attraction to God must echo this reality. While in the above descriptions I have mentioned some names of people who exemplify one of the traditional "four voices" of God, it is important to emphasize that in the case of the saints there is almost always a harmonious balance. They experience in their lives all "four voices," and thus provide us with inspiration.

A Hardened Heart

> I felt at the time that religion would impede my work. I wanted to have nothing to do with the religion of those I saw all around me. I felt that I must turn from it as from a drug. I felt it indeed to be an opiate of the people and not a very attractive one, so I hardened my heart. It was a conscious and deliberate process.[2]   *Dorothy Day*

Dorothy Day would eventually respond to God and soften her heart and become a world leader in the Church's work for the poor and the disenfranchised.

A hardened heart is one of the most problematic dilemmas that we can experience along our journey in life (cf. Jn 12:40). It is so problematic in that it is very difficult to overcome and to heal.

---

[2] Dorothy Day, *The Long Loneliness* (New York: Curtis Books, 1972), 10.

The Awakening

There is perhaps nothing more obtrusive to the gift of grace than a heart that is unwilling to open itself up to the possibility of an all-engulfing God.

A hardened heart is a frightened heart, a heart unwilling to take a chance at experiencing anything beyond its comfort level. There is a fear that what we may find if we open our heart will be too overwhelming to deal with.

A hardened heart is most often the consequence of some unresolved issue or deep psychological scar that has never been dealt with properly. We cannot conquer what we do not recognize.

When we examine the lives of atheists, it is astonishingly common to find these people lacking in good fatherly figures. It is difficult to pray "Our Father who art in heaven" when our only experience of a father has been that of one who was evil, mean-spirited, or non-existent. When looking at the lives of the world's major atheists, such as men like Nietzsche, we are struck by this lack of fatherly guidance. For people such as this, nothing short of a miracle is necessary to soften their hearts.

It is here where the communion of saints becomes so significant (cf. Jn 2:1-14; Rv 5:8). The communion of the faithful here on earth and in heaven has a profound effect on the softening of hearts throughout the world, for by themselves people with hardened hearts are much too weak to respond to the grace that is being showered upon them. A tragic event or the power of the prayers of the saints is often the only way these people soften their hearts. In many ways, they are very much like addicts. They often need to hit rock bottom before they can acknowledge the need of another. It is through the prayers of others, known and unknown, that the world's hearts are softened.

We must, thus, never underestimate the power of praying for others. St. Monica prayed for thirty years for the conversion of her son, Augustine. Her prayers were successful in softening his heart and he became the great St. Augustine.

2

Foundational Points

The Dignity of the Human Person

> Christ, …in the very revelation of the mystery of the Father and of his love, makes man fully manifest to himself and brings to light his exalted vocation.[3]

In Christ, "the image of the invisible God" (Col 1:15; cf. 2 Cor 4:4), the human person has been created in the "image and likeness of God." This image and likeness to God is seen in a person's expression of his or her powers of the intellect, will, and freedom.[4] It is in Christ, the Savior and Redeemer, that the divine image is ennobled.[5]

The human person is gifted with an immortal and spiritual nature. The human person is the only act of creation that God willed for its own unique sake.[6] From the very moment of conception, the human person is born to eternal life, eternal happiness.[7]

---

[3] GS 22.
[4] GS 17.
[5] GS 22.
[6] GS 24.
[7] CCC 1703.

The human person has been endowed with the gift of freely seeking and loving the good and the true. A person is endowed with the ability to perceive the good, the true, and the evil. It is a gift that is found at the very core of each and every person. It is a natural law that has been embedded into the core of a person's conscience.[8]

At the beginning of time humanity had a choice to live with God or live without him (cf. Gn 3:1-24). The choice to live without God caused a wound, a wound that has forever affected human nature. It is the wound that has come to be known as original sin, a sin of such a great nature that it destroyed the possibility of eternal life and happiness. Yet God would not allow humanity to remain separated from eternal life with him. He sent his only begotten Son to restore us to a new life in God (2 Cor 5:17). Sin was forgiven by the merits of Christ.

Yet even though the deep, penetrating cut of original sin was cleansed by the blood of Christ on the cross, a scar persisted, a scar called concupiscence. Thus, scarred, but not destroyed, human nature is forever tempted and inclined, on this earthly journey, toward evil and error.

Thus, human nature is involved in a spiritual battle, a battle between good and evil, light and darkness (cf. Jn 1:5; 8:12; 12:35).[9] It is a spiritual battle, however, that is fought with the gift of God's grace that was restored to us in Christ Jesus.

The gift of grace is that gift that enables us to become a child of God (cf. 1 Jn 5:1). Through the merits of Christ and the gift of grace, we are able to grow in the spiritual and moral life.[10]

---

[8] GS 15-17; CCC 1704-1707.
[9] GS 13; CCC 1706.
[10] CCC 1709.

Grace[11]

> Grace is… rooted in us, and worked into us like leaven, from our earliest years, until the thing thus present becomes fixed in a man like a natural endowment, as if it were one substance with him. But, for the man's own good, it manages him in many different ways, after its own pleasure. Sometimes the fire flames out and kindles more vehemently; at other times more gently and mildly. The light that it gives kindles up at times and shines with unusual brightness; at others it abates and burns low. The lamp is always burning and shining, but when it is specially trimmed, it kindles up with intoxication with the love of God….[12]
> *Pseudo-Macarius*

The Christian is one who responds to live life in love, the love of God, neighbor, and self (cf. Lk 10:27). The Christian is one who is moving toward total authenticity, toward total and full *human-ness*. The Christian is radically oriented to respond to his or her ultimate destiny of union with the self-communicating God of love. The spiritual journey is a call to be awakened, purified, and illuminated to one's true nature. The spiritual life is a call to reality, to see reality as it truly is and to see one's own self as one truly is.

Grace is the fundamental reality of the spiritual journey. Grace is a participation in the life of God, which justifies, sanctifies, deifies, and makes one a co-heir with God (cf. Jn 1:12-18; 17:3; Rm 8:14-17; 2 Cor 5:17-18; 2 P 1:3-4). Grace is the

---

[11] Cf. CCC 1996-2005. See Henri de Lubac, *A Brief Catechesis on Nature and Grace*, trans. Brother Richard Arnandez (San Francisco: Ignatius Press, 1984) for a historical survey of the relationship between nature and grace.

[12] *Fifty Spiritual Homilies of St. Macarius the Great*, trans. A.J. Mason (Willits: Eastern Orthodox Books, 1974), Homily VIII, n. 2.

gift of God himself — *the giver is the gift*.[13] Grace is a supernatural, gratuitous, and perfecting gift and favor that is always present — existentially present — at the very core of the person waiting to be accepted or rejected in freedom.[14] When a person truly seeks to understand his or her very core, he or she is bound to end up finding grace, finding God.

Habitual Grace

Habitual grace or sanctifying grace is that gift of the Holy Spirit that gives an individual the capacity to act in accordance with the demands of faith, hope and love. It is with the person, unless eliminated by mortal sin.[15]

Actual Graces

Flares of grace, divine touches, wounds of love, darts of love are often what are referred to as actual graces.[16] An actual grace is a gift, a special flare or moment of God's self-communicating, that enables a person to act in a salutary, beneficial, curative, and holy manner. Often this flare of grace is experienced as an interior impulse, attraction, inspiration, illumination, or interior light. At times it is experienced as a special moment of strength, courage or endurance. At other times it arouses good thoughts and feelings that seem to come from nowhere.[17]

---

[13] Karl Rahner, *Foundations of the Christian Faith: An Introduction to the Idea of Christianity*, trans. by William V. Dych (New York: Crossroad Publishing, Co., 1984), 120.

[14] Cf. Rahner, *Foundations*, 128.

[15] Cf. ST Ia, q. 105, a. 4; Ia IIae, q. 9, a. 6; q. 10, a. 4; q. 109, a. 2, 3, 4, 10. All quotations and citations regarding St. Thomas Aquinas' *Summa Theologiae* will always be cited in full in this text in order to alleviate confusion.

[16] Cf. *Spiritual Canticle*, St. 1, nos. 17-22; *Living Flame*, St. 1, no. 27. All quotations and citations from St. John of the Cross and St. Teresa of Avila are taken from the Institute of Carmelite Studies' editions.

[17] Cf. ST Ia, q. 105, a. 4; Ia IIae, q. 9, a. 6, q. 10, a. 4; q. 109, a. 2, 3, 4, 10.

Foundational Points

> The life of grace is a taste of heaven, for it is a taste of God.[18]
>
> St. Thomas Aquinas

Grace and Nature[19]

We are body and soul (cf. 1 Th 5:13; Mt 10:28). This reality has a profound impact on the spiritual life. If a person's body is healthy, psychologically and physically, grace has a much more profound impact on the spiritual life of the person, depending on the person's free-will response to God's self-communication. If, however, the body is ill, psychologically or physically, then the spiritual life is subject to difficulties in its progress. Likewise, if the person's spiritual life is weak, then a person's soul will be unhealthy, and so too will the body. The body will be subject to all kinds of psychological and related physical ailments. Hence, we are called to foster a healthy physical and spiritual life. If our bodily existence is ailing, we should seek all the medical attention within our capacity (e.g., medication, counseling, etc., cf. 1 Tm 5:23). If our spiritual life is unhealthy, we must seek a deeper conversion so as to promote a healthy bodily existence.

What about the cross? It is true that at times, despite all the medical attention we may have had access to, the body bears incurable wounds. This is the mystery of the cross and the mystery of grace. Despite it all, Christ, the *Great Physician*, takes the weaknesses and wounds of a person and elevates them into strengths: Who better to understand a person's weakness than one who is weak?

Grace not only builds upon nature, but it also heals and elevates it to new heights (cf. 2 Cor 12:10). Thus, grace is often the source of the healing of many ailments, whether physical or psychological.

---

[18] Cf. ST IIa IIae, q. 24, a. 3 ad 2um; Ia IIae, q. 69, a. 2.

[19] See de Lubac, *Nature and Grace*.

Grace and Merit

[Faith] apart from works is dead (cf. Jm 2:14-26).

Grace and good works are inseparable realities in the life of a person. Authentic faith always points to authentic holy works and authentically holy works are always marked by authentic faith. It is this reality between grace and merit that exemplifies the reality of the spiritual journey, since all are called to perfection (cf. Rm 8:28-30) and the spiritual battle (cf. 2 Tm 4).

Justification[20]

Justification flows from grace. Grace provides the person with the possibility of entering into the Paschal mystery — Jesus' life, death, resurrection and ascension. Consequently, grace justifies a person. It makes one a "new creation" in God (cf. Rm 3:22; 6:3-4, 8-11; 1 Cor 12; Jn 15:1-4).

There are essentially six key aspects in regard to justification:

1) "Justification is not only the remission of sins, but also the sanctification and renewal of the interior man," conversion (cf. Mt 4:17).[21]
2) Justification detaches a person from sin, from enslavement, through the continual offer of forgiveness. It reconciles and heals the person's innermost being.
3) Justification is the acceptance of God's righteousness. It is the acceptance of the life of faith, hope, and love — a life in obedience to God's will.
4) Justification has been merited by Christ's Passion (cf. Rm 3:21-26). Justification implies a blood atonement for sins and the gift of eternal life through the gift of baptism into Christ's

---

[20] Cf. CCC 1987-1995.
[21] Council of Trent (1547): DS 1528.

life, death, and resurrection (either by a baptism of desire, blood, or water).
5) Justification establishes the cooperation between grace and freedom. On God's part there is the continual offer of grace. On the person's part there is the demand for continual conversion (cf. Mt 4:17) and the continual assent to faith. It demands response to the Spirit and cooperation in divine love.
6) Justification entails the sanctification of the whole being (cf. Rm 6:19, 22).

The Moral Law[22]

The moral law is that which guides us on the spiritual journey. There are three kinds of moral laws, all of which are interrelated, and all of which find their source of being at the core of the person (cf. Ph 2:12-13).

Natural Law

Natural law finds its impetus in God's wisdom and thus the immutable gift of reason.[23] The goal of the moral law is life in Christ (cf. Rm 10:4).

> The natural law is written and engraved in the soul of each and every man, because it is human reason ordaining him to do good and forbidding him to sin.... But this command of human reason would not have the force of law if it were not the voice and interpreter of a higher reason to which our spirit and our freedom must be submitted.[24]
> *Leo XIII*

---

[22] Cf. CCC 1950-1974; 2031-2046.
[23] Cf. GS 10.
[24] Leo XIII, *Libertas praestantissimum*, 597, quoted in CCC 1954.

Where then are these rules written, if not in the book of that light we call the truth? In it is written every just law; from it the law passes into the heart of the man who does justice, not that it migrates into it, but that it places its imprint on it, like a seal on a ring that passes unto wax, without leaving the ring.[25]   *St. Augustine*

The natural law is nothing other than the light of understanding in us by God; through it we know what we must do and what we must avoid. God has given this light or law at creation.[26]   *St. Thomas Aquinas*

Through the natural law we practice that which is good and attend to our eternal destiny, our salvation.[27] The natural law promotes the dignity and the rights and duties of the person.

Revealed Law

Divine revelation, which is found in the Sacred Scriptures and Sacred Tradition, reveals that which is in the heart.[28] It aids, enlightens, and clarifies the natural moral law, which sin can often cloud.[29] The moral law finds its fulfillment in the law of love.

Ecclesiastical Law

The laws or precepts of the Church nourish and strengthen a person's ability to perceive and follow the innate natural law. The emphasis on these laws is on attending Mass on a regular basis, receiving communion, seeking reconciliation, fasting and abstain-

---

[25] St. Augustine, *De Trin.* 14, 15, 21: PL 42, 1052.
[26] St. Thomas Aquinas, *Dec. praec.* I.
[27] Cf. GS 89.
[28] St. Augustine, *En. In* Ps 57, 1: PL 36, 673.
[29] Pius XII, *Humani generis*: DS 3876; cf. *Dei Filius* 2: DS 3005.

ing from meat on appointed days, joining in the missionary efforts of the Church, and so on.

The Moral Virtues

> To live well is nothing other than to love God with all one's heart, with all one's soul and with all one's efforts; from this it comes about that love is kept whole and uncorrupted (through temperance). No misfortune can disturb it (and this is fortitude). It obeys only [God] (and this is justice), and is careful in discerning things, so as not to be surprised by deceit or trickery (and this is prudence).[30]
>
> *St. Augustine*

A holy person is a virtuous person (cf. Ws 8:7; Ph 4:8). A holy person is a virtuous person who seeks "to be like God"[31]; that is, to be in the image and likeness to which he or she was originally created in (cf. Gn 1:27). Therefore, in order for one to comprehend the path that grace draws one toward, one needs to comprehend the virtues. There are two types of virtues, the acquired moral virtues and the infused moral virtues.

Acquired Moral Virtues

The acquired moral virtues are acquired by the repetition of acts under the direction of the light of *natural right reason*. Grace is not required to acquire these natural virtues. In fact, one can in theory be a person in a state of mortal sin and still be considered somewhat virtuous. For example, a man in a state of mortal sin

---

[30] St. Augustine, *De moribus eccl.* 1, 25, 46: PL 32, 1330-1331.
[31] St. Gregory of Nyssa, *De beatitudinibus*, 1: PG 44, 1200D.

may seek sobriety in order to live a reasonable and productive life. Right reason directs this man. While such a person in mortal sin may have some qualities that may be called virtuous, such a person inevitably lacks the moral integration that the virtues in combination bring about.

Furthermore, such people may often appear to be virtuous when in fact they are simply being self-centered. This has traditionally been called "false virtue." For example, a person may seem to be guiding his or her life according to right reason, when in fact such a person is guiding his or her life according to some other factor such as the desire for fame, money, power, etc. Or a man may choose to run into a burning building to save some helpless elderly woman. On the surface one would say that that person had the virtue of courage. However, if that person ran into the building with a secret agenda of becoming famous or a hero, then this is no longer an act of virtue but an act of self-aggrandizement. It is an act of "false virtue."[32]

Infused Moral Virtues

Infused moral virtues require a person's response to grace. Through a person's response to grace, the acquired virtues, which are guided by right reason, are elevated to a level that surpasses the limits of right reason alone. Only God can empower a person with infused moral virtues. They are by nature supernatural acts of grace. These virtues are directed toward a person's supernatural last end and consequently are essential for eternal life.[33]

---

[32] Cf. ST Ia IIae, q. 49, a. 2; q. 65, a. 2.
[33] Cf. ST Ia IIae, q. 63, a. 3, 4; q. 109, a. 3.

*The Relationship Between Acquired
and Infused Moral Virtues*

Holiness at whatever level requires the proper interaction of the acquired and infused moral virtues.[34] The proper interaction of the acquired moral virtues and the infused moral virtues make for the perfect spiritual person. In such a case, all of a person's life is in perfect harmony, like five fingers on a hand.[35]

The Theological Virtues (cf. 1 Cor 13:13)

The theological virtues of faith, hope, and love empty a person of all that is not for the honor and glory of God and fills such a person with God's self-communicating, cleansing presence. A person is empty to be filled. The human virtues are grounded in the theological virtues (cf. 2 P 1:4), which enable a person to be animated, informed, and enlivened in Christ. Faith frees the intellect to soar into realms of knowing it had never before experienced (Is 55:8-9). It penetrates the deep mysteries of God that are beyond the natural and rational boundaries.[36] Hope empties the memory of the unhealthy, worldly passing allurements that seek to compete with the bliss that comes from God. Love unburdens the will and the heart of all that is false and fleeting and helps one to cling to that which is of God.[37] In faith, hope, and love one moves toward union with God, one moves toward peace, happiness, and light.[38]

---

[34] Cf. ST IIa IIae, q. 24, a. 9.
[35] Cf. ST Ia IIae, q. 66, a. 2.
[36] Cf. *Ascent*, Bk. II, Ch. 1, no. 1.
[37] Cf. *Ascent*, Bk. II, Ch. 6, nos. 1-4.
[38] Cf. *Ascent*, Bk. II, Ch. 4, nos. 2-3.

Gifts of the Spirit

The gifts of the Holy Spirit are essential to the spiritual growth of the person and are essential for salvation.[39] The gifts of the Spirit are what transform a hardened heart into a docile heart, a heart ready for God's engulfing presence.[40] Knowledge, understanding, wisdom, counsel, piety, fortitude, and fear of the Lord are the traditional gifts of the Spirit (Is 11:2f). The gift of knowledge helps us to understand God's creation; the gift of understanding helps us to delve into the sphere of truth; the gift of wisdom, the highest of the gifts, aids us to perceive the divine; the gift of counsel helps us to direct our actions according to God's will; the gift of piety aids us in proper worship; the gift of fortitude helps us fight off the fears that confront us in the works of God; and the gift of fear of the Lord protects us from falling into disorderly temptations.

The Evangelical Counsels

The evangelical counsels are poverty, chastity, and obedience. They lead to spiritual perfection and the healing of moral wounds. Poverty is empowered by the theological virtue of hope, chastity by the theological virtue of love, and obedience by the theological virtue of faith. The counsels, thus, render to God what is due to him.[41]

---

[39] Cf. ST Ia IIae, q. 68, a. 2.
[40] Cf. ST Ia IIae, q. 68, a. 3.
[41] Cf. ST Ia IIae, q. 108, a. 4; IIa IIae, q. 186, a. 3, 4, 5, 7.

The Beatitudes (Mt 5:3-12)

The beatitudes flow from the gifts of the Spirit and dispose a person to obey these gifts.[42] The beatitude of the "poor in spirit" promotes confidence in God and complete dependence on God (cf. Is 61:1; Zp 2:3). It also engenders a humble predisposition. The beatitude of the "mournful" is that beatitude which fosters recognition of God's consolation and comfort. The beatitude of the "meek" engenders the recognition of one's place in the kingdom of God (cf. Ps 37:11). The beatitude of "those who hunger and thirst for righteousness" promotes conformity to God's will and a willing submission to God's plan of salvation for all. The beatitude of the "merciful" properly orders the virtue of justice in accordance to the "spirit of the law" as opposed to the "letter of the law." The beatitude of the "pure of heart" is that assurance that God's presence will always be with one whose heart is clean (cf. Ps 24:4; 42:3). The beatitude of the "peacemakers" is one that promotes peace in one's heart and in the hearts of others. It promotes a docile, gentle spirit that is ordered to the providential plan of God. The beatitude of the unjustly "persecuted" is that beatitude which empowers one to seek justice at whatever cost, even at the cost of one's life. To live the life of the beatitudes is to live the life that brings one to experience the ultimate in happiness in a world filled with trials and tribulations.

The beatitudes express the human person's vocation as a spiritual being. They shed light on a Christian's duties and attitudes. They sustain hope amidst a world of trials and tribulations.[43] They "proclaim the blessings and rewards already secured, however dimly, for Christ's disciples."[44]

---

[42] Cf. ST Ia IIae, q. 70, a. 2.
[43] CCC 1717.
[44] Ibid.

The beatitudes express a person's innermost desire, that person's desire for happiness. This desire for happiness has been placed at the very core of the human person in order to draw him or her to God, the source of all happiness.[45]

> We all want to live happily; in the whole human race there is no one who does not assent to this proposition, even before it is fully articulated.[46]   *St. Augustine*
>
> How is it, then, I seek you, Lord? Since in seeking you, my God, I seek a happy life, let me seek you so that my soul may live, for my body draws life from my soul and my soul draws life from you.[47]   *St. Augustine*
>
> God alone satisfies.[48]   *St. Thomas Aquinas*

St. Thomas Aquinas says that another word for God is "happiness." The sad reality of life is that many people today, as in all generations, have failed to recognize that God alone is happiness and that God alone satisfies. Such people, sadly, end up chasing after things that appear at first sight to bring about happiness but in the end these "things" only bring about disappointment. Some people seek to fill this innate desire for happiness with fame, power, human achievement, drugs, disordered sex, and so forth, yet they never find peace and contentment.

> All bow down before wealth. Wealth is that to which the multitude of men pay an instinctive homage. They measure happiness by wealth; and by wealth they measure respectability.... It is a homage resulting from a profound faith... that with wealth he may do all things. Wealth is

---

[45] CCC 1718.
[46] St. Augustine, *De moribus eccl.* 1, 3, 4: PL 32, 1312.
[47] St. Augustine, *Confessions*, 10, 20: PL 32, 791.
[48] St. Thomas Aquinas, *Expos. In symb. Apost.* I.

> one idol of the day and notoriety is a second.... Notoriety, or the making of a noise in the world — it may be called "newspaper fame" — has come to be considered a great good in itself, and a ground of veneration.[49]
>
> John Henry Newman

If only people could recognize what the great saints have always recognized: That our soul will only rest in God (cf. Ps 62:1).

The beatitudes challenge and confront people. They force people to make choices regarding their eternal destiny.

Freedom, Responsibility, and Personal Becoming

> Man is rational and therefore like God; he is created with free will and is master over his acts.[50]

At the core of a person's nature or essence, intrinsic to him or her, is that person's freedom. Freedom is the means by which a person primarily becomes something. A person is so free that he or she has within his or her being the capacity to take control of his or her basic nature. A person is able to determine what he or she is and what he or she is to be. Therefore, at the heart of the definition of the person is the reality that the person is one who is open to becoming.[51]

Freedom is an openness to that which is beyond — a movement toward fulfillment. Because freedom is open and a movement toward fulfillment it allows for self-causation, that is, the

---

[49] John Henry Newman, "Saintliness the Standard of Christian Principle," in *Discourses to Mixed Congregations* (London: Longmans, Green and Co., 1906), V, 89-90.

[50] St. Irenaeus, *Adv. Haeres.* 4, 4, 3: PG 7/1, 983.

[51] Cf. Karl Rahner, *Hearers of the Word*, trans. Michael Richards (New York: Herder and Herder, 1969), 3-179.

power to become. Freedom entails a possibility for self-achievement, self-becoming. In freedom we can realize our potential. In the words of Karl Rahner,

> ...[Freedom] is a permanent constituent of man's nature. The true nature of freedom appears precisely in this, that in the Christian revelation it is the cause of both absolute salvation and absolute rejection by the final judgment of God.... In the Christian view... man is, through his freedom, capable of determining.... Through his free decision he is rather truly good or evil in the very ground of his being, and thus, in the Christian view, his final salvation or loss is already present, even though perhaps still hidden.[52]

The person endowed with grace is on a journey — whether he is aware of it or not — toward the perfection of Christ, the God-man, the fully divine, fully human being. By seeking the God that dwells within, one can find one's true human potential, and by seeking to find one's full humanity, one can find the divine within whether in an explicit way or an implicit way.[53]

Christians are called into the *Mystery of God*. By making the choice to enter into this mystery one is making a choice to enter into the spiritual life, the beginning of the mystical life.[54]

The Limitations of Human Freedom

Human freedom is not absolute. It is limited and subject to errors. It is limited in that it demands obedience to the natural law that resides at the core of every person, and it is subject to

---

[52] Karl Rahner, *Grace in Freedom*, trans. Hilda Graef (New York: Herder and Herder, 1969), 210-211.
[53] Cf. Rahner, *Foundations*, 1-459.
[54] Cf. Karl Rahner, *Theology of Renewal*, trans. Cecily Hastings (New York: Sheed and Ward, 1964), 73.

error in that it is subject to the slavery and blindness that is associated with sin. As the *Catechism* states, "By deviating from the moral law man violates his own freedom, becomes imprisoned within himself, disrupts neighborly fellowship, and rebels against divine truth."[55] Human history attests to the sad consequences that result from the sinful abuse of freedom.

The Christian is called to live a life in imitation of Christ. The Savior who saved us from the slavery of sin is the one that all are called to imitate, for in this imitation is found the ultimate in liberation and freedom (cf. Gal 5:1; Jn 8:32; 2 Cor 17; Rm 8:21). In the grace of Christ one is educated and nourished in the ways of authentic freedom.[56]

In the early stages of the spiritual journey, the imitation of Christ is quite difficult, and therefore one's sense of freedom and liberation is curtailed.

Moral Conscience

> Deep within his conscience man discovers a law which he has not laid upon himself but which he must obey. Its voice, ever calling him to love and to do what is good and to avoid evil, sounds in his heart at the right moment.... For man has in his heart a law inscribed by God.... His conscience is man's most secret core and his sanctuary. There he is alone with God whose voice echoes in his depths.[57]
> *Gaudium et Spes*

A person entrusted with this innate moral law, this conscience, is obliged to be faithful to this moral law in choosing what

---

[55] CCC 1740.
[56] CCC 1741-1742.
[57] GS 16; Cf. Rm 1:32; 2:14-16. All quotes and references from Scripture are from the RSV.

is right and just. In so doing one recognizes the ultimate in truth, truth itself, God himself, Christ himself.

> Conscience is a messenger of him, who, both in nature and in grace, speaks to us behind a veil, and teaches and rules us by his representatives. Conscience is the aboriginal Vicar of Christ.[58]   *John Henry Newman*

Conscience directs us to conversion and to hope. It enables us to recognize the evil we have done and consequently to ask for God's forgiveness. Conscience also helps us recognize the good and the power of hope. It directs us away from evil, unhappiness, despair, and moves us toward happiness, peace, and light.

The Formation of Conscience

We have a moral obligation to form our conscience in accordance to right reason and the will of God. It is a lifelong task. In the purgative stage of spirituality, the conscience is often poorly formed, while in the succeeding stages the conscience becomes more enlightened. The following are some general guidelines for the proper formation of our conscience:

- Reflection, self-examination, and introspection make up the ground level of an informed conscience.
- Absorption in the Word of God (Ps 119:105) and Sacred Tradition (the life of the Holy Spirit within the Church) serve as the blood of life for the conscience.
- The authoritative teachings of the Church that flow from Sacred Scripture and Sacred Tradition are essential (cf. 2 Th 2:15).

---

[58] John Henry Newman, "Letter to the Duke of Norfolk," V, in *Certain Difficulties felt by Anglicans in Catholic Teaching* II (London: Longmans Green, 1885), 248.

Foundational Points

- Reading the spiritual masters and the advice of good spiritual directors are extremely helpful in putting all the above into a concise vision of reality that corresponds to the innate reality at the core of a person's being.

A well-formed conscience engenders freedom and peace of heart.

Determining a Well-Informed Conscience

There are essentially two key guides that help us to determine if we have a well-informed conscience:
1) A good end does not justify an evil means.
2) Do unto others as you would like done unto you (cf. Mt 7:12; Lk 6:31; Rm 14:21; 1 Cor 8:12; Tb 4:15).

An Uninformed Conscience[59]

> Like all things human, even [the] conscience can fail to …[perceive] illusions and errors. It is a delicate voice that can be overpowered by a noisy, distracted way of life, or almost suffocated by a long-lasting and serious habit of sin.[60]
> *Pope John Paul II*

There are two main reasons for an uninformed conscience:
1) The propensity toward laziness is at the heart of those who fail to seek a well-informed conscience.
2) A sinful life often blinds us to recognize the truth and often deadens our conscience.

> The more correct conscience prevails, the more do persons and groups turn aside from blind choice and try to be guided by objective standards of moral conduct.[61]
> *Gaudium et Spes*

---

[59] GS 16.
[60] John Paul II, *Celebrate 2000: Reflections on Jesus, the Holy Spirit, and the Father* (Ann Arbor: Servant Publications, 1996), 151.
[61] GS 16.

An Examination of Conscience

An examination of conscience is a powerful way of keeping our conscience informed and open to the working of grace. The following is a general method of examining our conscience: We must first begin by praying to God for enlightenment. We must then ask ourselves the following key questions: "Who am I as God sees me? What is happening in my life at this moment? How is God working in me? How is evil working in me? What is God asking of me? What would Jesus do in my situation?" From these key questions flows a profound examination of conscience.

Original and Personal Sin

Original Sin

> There is nothing upon earth which does not demonstrate either the misery of man or the mercy of God; either the powerlessness of man without God — or his power in union with God…. Man does not know where he belongs. He has obviously gone astray and has fallen from his proper place. He cannot find his way back to it, though he seeks it everywhere in great anxiety but without success, moving about in impenetrable darkness….[62]   *Blaise Pascal*

There are three competing theories to describe the creation or evolution of man and woman. Some argue for the theory of *creationism*, which maintains that God created man and woman without the necessity of an evolutionary process. There is the theory of *atheistic evolution* which maintains that human life

---
[62] *The Essential Pascal*, sel. and ed. Robert W. Gleason, S.J., and trans. G.F. Pullen (New York: New American Library, 1966), 69f.

Foundational Points

evolved from lower forms to higher forms by a random process. Finally, there is the theory of *theistic evolution*, the belief that God created the world out of nothing and that he guided the evolutionary process from a lower form of life to a higher form of life, until he finally placed an immortal soul into the first human beings. Such a belief was embraced by the Jesuit priest and anthropologist, Pierre Teilhard de Chardin, who saw evolution as compatible with Christianity in that he saw all things evolving toward the perfection of Christ.

> Lord Jesus Christ you truly contain within your gentleness, within your humanity, all the unyielding immensity and grandeur of the world.
> You are the center at which all things meet and which stretches out over all things so as to draw them back into itself; I love you for the extension of your body and soul to the farthest corners of creation through grace, through life, and through matter.
> Lord Jesus, you who are as gentle as the human heart, as fiery as the forces of nature, as intimate as life itself, you in whom I can melt away and with whom I must have mastery and freedom; I love you as a world, as this world which has captivated my heart....
> Lord Jesus, you are the center towards which all things are moving.[63]

As Catholics, we can believe in a form of *creationism* or we can believe in *theistic evolution* as understood here. We cannot believe, however, in *atheistic evolution*, for it denies God's creative power and his providential will.

We may wonder how the belief in *theistic evolution* can be

---

[63] Pierre Teilhard de Chardin, "Cosmic Life" in *Writings in Time of War*, 69-70.

believed in terms of the account of creation in the book of Genesis. First and foremost, Genesis is not an historical account of the way the world began, nor the way human life began. All we need to do is compare Genesis 1 with Genesis 2:4f. Here, within the first two chapters of Genesis, we find two different accounts of creation. It is obvious that Genesis was not meant to be a literal historical account of how human beings came into being.

The book of Genesis is a theological account teaching us that God is the ultimate source of being. He created the world and people out of nothing. He created them good. It is an account of freedom and the cost of using freedom in a negative manner. It is an account of human individuals who chose to rebel against God and sought to live without God. By their sin they forever distorted the nature of the world. Genesis is the Word of God told to people thousands of years ago about the eternal truth of God, a God of mercy and love, a God of second chances.

Concupiscence

Original sin distorted the harmony of creation and damaged the relationship between God and humanity. The second Person of the Trinity, the Son of God, came into the world and cleansed it of this damage, this original sin. While the sin is forgiven in Christ, the wound remains.

Human beings, while in Christ, in God, are capable of an intimate, personal, saving relationship with God, and are capable of experiencing eternal life with God in heaven. Yet despite this, because of the wound of original sin, a human being is still inclined and tempted toward that original rebellion; that is, human beings are inclined toward the temptations of evil. The spiritual journey becomes a battle against concupiscence.

Foundational Points

Personal Sin

Sin is a personal act in which reason, truth, and right conscience are offended. It is a failure to live up to the command of love of God and neighbor caused by a perverse attachment to that which is not for the honor and glory of God. It is an act of self-infatuation, disobedience (Gn 3:5) and hatred toward God (Ps 51:4).[64] It wounds the nature of the human person, the nature of solidarity, and the nature of the eternal law.[65]

Kinds of Sin[66]

Sin comes from the heart, from the core of a person's very being (cf. Mt 15:19-20). The two main kinds of sins are sins of commission and sins of omission. Sins of commission are sins in which a person takes an active part — such as acts of fornication, impurity, licentiousness, idolatry, sorcery, enmity, strife, jealousy, anger, selfishness, dissension, envy, drunkenness, carousing, etc. (cf. Gal 5:19-21; Rm 1:28-32; 1 Cor 9-10; Eph 5:3-5; Col 3:5-8; 1 Tm 9-10; 2 Tm 2-5). Sins of omission are sins that involve actions that are omitted in fostering the glory and honor of God. These are sins committed by people who keep quiet when evil is being done. People who do nothing to put an end to abortion and euthanasia, for example, are the quintessential type of people who commit serious sins of omission. These people can be equated to the people who did nothing to put an end to slavery in the United States' early history. They did nothing to put an end to evil. Failing to stop gossip, vulgarity, and so forth, are other forms of sins of omission.

---

[64] St. Augustine, *De civ. Dei* 14, 28: PL 41, 436.
[65] St. Augustine, *Contra Faustum* 22: PL 42, 418.
[66] Cf. CCC 1849-1850.

Gravity of Sin[67]

> If anyone sees his brother committing what is not a mortal sin, he will ask, and God will give him life for those whose sin is not mortal. There is sin which is mortal.... All wrongdoing is sin, but there is sin which is not mortal (2 Jn 5:16-17).

There are mortal/deadly sins and there are venial/non-deadly sins. Mortal sin involves the loss of sanctifying grace and love. It is a radical rejection of God, a radical turning away from God. Mortal sin leads to hell. On the other hand, venial or non-deadly sins do not deprive one of heaven. In venial sin love remains, though it is offended and damaged.

In order to commit a mortal sin one needs to take into account the following conditions:

1) The sin must be one that involves a *grave matter*. Traditionally grave matter has been associated with the gross violation of the Ten Commandments.
2) Full knowledge and sufficiently deliberate consent is needed in the committing of a sin.
3) Unintentional ignorance (not feigned ignorance or hardness of heart) diminishes or removes the seriousness of the sin (i.e., pathological disorders, inordinate feelings and passions).

Venial sin is sin that does not meet the above requirements. Venial sin weakens love, disorders affections for created things, hinders virtuous progress, and disposes one toward mortal sin by damaging the conscience. Yet venial sin does not break a person's covenant or friendship with God. It does not deprive one of sanctifying grace nor of heaven.

---

[67] Cf. CCC 1854-1864.

Foundational Points

> While he is in the flesh, man cannot help but have at least some light sins. Despise these sins which we call "light": if you take them for light when you weigh them, tremble when you count them. A number of light objects make a great mass; a number of drops fill a river; a number of grains make a heap. What then is our hope? Above all, confession....[68]
> *St. Augustine*

Communal Nature of Spirituality[69]

> [An error,] today abundantly widespread, is disregard for the law of human solidarity and charity, dictated and imposed both by our common origin and by the equality in the rational nature of all men, whatever nation they belong to. This law is sealed by the sacrifice of redemption offered by Jesus Christ on the altar on the Cross to his heavenly Father, on behalf of sinful humanity.[70]
> *Pius XII*

The love of God and the love of neighbor are inseparable realities. To authentically love God we must authentically love our neighbor, and to authentically love our neighbor we need to authentically love God.

The communal nature of spirituality promotes the common good of society, which promotes the defense of the fundamental rights of persons, the development of spirituality, and peace and security. Any form of sinful inequality is condemned.

---

[68] St. Augustine, *In ep. Jo.* 1, 6: PL 35, 1982.
[69] Cf. CCC 1878-1880; 1928-1942.
[70] Pius XII, *Summi pontificatus*, October 20, 1939; AAS 31 (1939) 423ff.

Sin and Mercy[71]

All people fall short of the perfection of Christ and therefore sin is a cancer that engulfs this world (cf. Rm 5:12). Yet despite this sad reality, God's mercy never leaves a person. Even a mortal sin does not withdraw God's divine mercy from the core of the person,[72] for if it did, there would be no possibility of repentance, forgiveness and conversion.[73]

The Seven Capital Sins and Their Vices

The capital sins are commonly found in the purgative stage of the spiritual journey. They are often mortal, but not at all times.[74] As a consequence of original sin, we are susceptible to capital sins and their vices. A capital sin leads us to separation from God and all kinds of other sins. They also lead from lesser sins to more serious ones.

The following is a brief description of the seven capital sins and what is often born of them: The capital sin of envy gives life to hatred, slander, calumny, detraction, and joy at the misfortune of others. Anger leads to disputes, fits of passion, insults, blasphemy, rudeness, haughtiness, and contempt. Vanity leads to disobedience, boasting, hypocrisy, unholy rivalry, discord, and stubbornness. Sloth (or acedia) gives rise to malice, rancor, discour-

---

[71] Cf. CCC 1846-1848; Cf. Lk 15.
[72] ST Ia IIae, q. 88, a. 2.
[73] It has been argued by some people that a God of love could never allow for any person to be condemned to hell for eternity. The answer to this point is found in the very nature of love itself. Authentic love always implies justice. A loving God is a God of justice. If it did not matter whether a person was evil or good, and that all went to heaven, then God would be unjust. Justice demands that those who choose to live evilly are to receive their just rewards.
[74] *Dark Night*, Bk. I, Ch. 208.

agement, cowardliness, spiritual apathy or stagnation, forgetfulness of spiritual obligations, and the seeking after forbidden things. Avarice gives rise to disloyalty, treachery, fraud, deceit, perjury, harshness, hardness of heart, and an excessive desire for acquiring and maintaining things. Gluttony leads one to engage in improper jokes, coarse and loutish behavior, impurity, foolish conversation, and stupidity. Lust gives rise to spiritual blindness, poor judgment, impetuous or rash decisions, fickleness, instability, capriciousness, self-infatuation, and an inordinate attachment to this present life.[75]

Prayer in General

> Prayer is the fruit of joy and thanksgiving and the ascent of the person's very being to God.[76]   *Evagrius Ponticus*

> For me prayer is a surge of the heart; it is a simple look turned toward heaven; it is a cry of recognition and of love, embracing both trials and joy.[77]   *St. Thérèse of Lisieux*

Prayer as Gift

"Prayer is the raising of one's mind and heart to God or the requesting of good things from God."[78] Prayer is founded upon humility and a contrite heart (Ps 130:1; cf. Lk 18:9-14). We must recognize that we need help in the endeavor of prayer (Rm 8:26) and we must recognize that "whether we realize it or not, prayer

---

[75] Cf. ST Ia IIae, q. 77, a. 4f; q. 84, a. 4.
[76] Evagrius Ponticus, *The 153 Chapters on Prayer*, 15, 35.
[77] St. Thérèse of Lisieux, *Manuscrits autobiographiques*, C 25r.
[78] St. John Damascene, *De fide orth.* 3, 24: PG 94, 1098C; CCC 2559.

is an encounter of God's thirst with ours. God thirsts that we may thirst for him" (cf. Jn 4:10).[79] "Prayer is the response of faith to the free promise of salvation and also a response of love to the thirst of the only Son of God" (cf. Jn 7:37-39; 19:28; Is 12:3; 51:1; Zc 12:10; 13:1).[80]

Prayer as Covenant

When we pray, we pray with our heart, which is the dwelling place where we are, where we live, where we withdraw to. The heart is

> our hidden center, beyond the grasp of our reason and of others; only the Spirit of God can fathom the human heart and know it fully. The heart is the place of decision, deeper than our psychic drives. It is the place of truth, where we choose life or death. It is the place of encounter, because as image of God we live in relation; it is the place of covenant.[81]

Prayer is a committed relationship of life and love. It is meant to be an inseparable relationship of encounter between the Creator and his creation.

Prayer as Communion

Prayer is a communion between the individual, God, and his Body the Church. While one may invoke each person of the Trinity and pray to each person of the Trinity, it is traditionally understood that prayer is directed toward the Father, through the

---

[79] Cf. St. Augustine, *De diversis quaestionibus octoginta tribus* 54, 4: PL 40, 56; CCC 2560.
[80] CCC 2561.
[81] CCC 2563.

Son, and in the Holy Spirit in a mystical community called the Church, the Church on earth, in purgatory, and in heaven. "In the Holy Spirit, Christian prayer is a communion of love with the Father, not only through Christ, but also *in him*...."[82]

Jesus and Prayer

Jesus teaches us to pray and reminds us that he prays for us, in us, and with us. As St. Augustine summarizes:

> He prays for us as our priest, prays in us as our Head, and is prayed to by us as our God. Therefore let us acknowledge our voice in him and his in us.[83]

From the Sermon on the Mount we are taught that prayer to the Father requires a conversion of the heart. Reconciliation, love of enemies, prayers for persecutors, attentive prayer, purity of heart, and the seeking of the kingdom are all at the core of a conversion of the heart (cf. Mt 5:23-24, 44-45; 6:7, 14-15, 21, 25, 33).

This conversion of heart leads to praying in faith, an adherence to God beyond what is limited to feelings and understanding. In faith we can therefore be assured of our access to the Father and the assurance that if we *seek* and *knock* we will receive answers, for Christ is the *door* and the *way* (Mt 7:7-11, 13-14). We can be confident that whatever we ask for in prayer and in faith will be received (Mk 11:24). We are reminded that in Jesus "all things are possible to those who believe" (Mk 9:23; cf. Mt 21:22).

It is important to remember, however, that an authentic prayer of faith is always one that is embodied by a heart disposed to do the will of the Father. Simply crying out, "Lord, Lord...,"

---

[82] CCC 2615.
[83] St. Augustine, *En. In Ps 85*, 1: PL 37, 1081; cf. GILH 7: CCC 2616.

is of little benefit if our heart is far from the will of God (cf. Mt 7:21). An authentic prayer of faith embodies the divine plan of God within it (cf. Mt 9:38; Lk 10:2; Jn 4:34). It realizes the importance of struggle and patience and perseverance (cf. Lk 18:1-8). Therefore, prayer is inseparable from works. In the words of Thomas Merton, prayer

> is inseparable from life and from the dynamism of life — which includes work, creation, production, fruitfulness, and above all love.... It is the very fullness of a fully integrated life. It is the crown of life and of all life's activities.[84]

Mary

> Mary, Mother of Jesus and of those who participate in his priestly ministry, we come to you with the same attitude of children who come to their mother. We are no longer children, but adults who desire with all our hearts to be God's children. Our human condition is weak; that is why we come to ask for your motherly aid so we are able to overcome our weakness. Pray for us so that we can, in turn, become people of prayer. We invoke your protection so that we may remain free from all sin. We invoke your love so that it may reign and we will be able to be compassionate and forgiving. We ask for your blessing so we can be like the image of your beloved Son, our Lord and Savior, Jesus Christ. Amen.[85]

May the Virgin make our hearts humble and submissive like her son's heart. In her the heart of Jesus was formed.

---

[84] *A Thomas Merton Reader*, Revised Edition. Edited by Thomas O. McDonnell (New York: Image Books, 1974), 400.

[85] Mother Teresa, *In My Own Words: Special Memorial Edition* (Liguori: Liguori Publications, 1996), 61.

> Let us learn to be humble, accepting humiliations with joy. We have been created for great things — why then should we stoop to things that would blur the beauty of our heart? How many things we can learn from the Virgin! Ask the Virgin to tell Jesus, "They have no more wine" — the wine of humility and submission, of goodness, of sweetness.... Ask Jesus to help you personalize your love for Mary — in order to be sources of joy, as he is; in order to be closer to her, as he is; in order to share with her everything, even the cross. Every one of us must carry his or her own cross; it is our sign of belonging to Christ. We need Mary to help us share it.[86]
> *Mother Teresa*

Mary's intercessory prayers have a unique role in the plan of salvation. At the Annunciation her prayer opened the way for Christ's conception (cf. Lk 1:38); at Pentecost her prayer helped form the Church (Ac 1:14). In her *fiat*, she was the perfect disciple, the perfect model of the Church; she was what all are called to be: "Behold I am the handmaid of the Lord; let it be done to me according to your word" (Lk 1:38). This is at the heart of Christian prayer: "to be wholly God's, because he is wholly ours."[87]

Mary teaches a person how to pray by her example of humility, love, obedience, faith, and trust.

Mary's intercessory power is unique for she is the Mother of God, the spouse of the Holy Spirit. At the wedding feast of Cana (Jn 2:1-12) the wine ran out. Jesus was not prepared to begin his public ministry. Yet when Mary, his mother, asked her Son to help the wedding couple — when Mary interceded — Jesus listened to the intercession of his mother and performed the miracle of turning water into wine. Mary's intercessory power is

---

[86] Mother Teresa, *Heart of Joy: The Transforming of Self-Giving* (Ann Arbor: Servant Books, 1987), 80-81; 139.
[87] CCC 2617.

in her nature as the Mother of the Lord, for what good son can refuse the request of a good mother?

Jesus himself reminds all of us to have recourse to Mary at the foot of the cross when he turns over to John and the whole world Mary as our Mother, as the New Eve, as the Daughter of Zion, as the Mother of the Church.

> When Jesus saw his mother, and the disciple whom he loved standing near, he said to his mother, "Woman, behold, your son!" Then he said to the disciple, "Behold, your mother!" (Jn 19:26)

Mary is our Mother. Christ gave the world a powerful intercessor for the needs of his people. Christ came into the world through Mary, and we are blessed to go to Jesus through Mary. Because we pray in the power of the Holy Spirit and the Mother of God is the spouse of the Holy Spirit, Mary becomes an essential part in Catholic spirituality.

It is important to recognize that Jesus could have entered the scene of history by simply walking out from the desert without any known origin, yet he chose a mother to enter the world, a mother from whom he took his flesh, a mother whom he listened to and loved. He never ceases to listen to her and to love her.

Mary never ceases to pray for us, now, and at the hour of our death!

The Church — A Communion

The Scriptures are clear on the necessity of interceding on behalf of others (cf. Lk 16:9; 1 Cor 12:12, 20f, 12:26; Heb 12:22f; Rv 5:8). The apostles often make reference to the need of praying for others and the need of the prayers of others. God intended this so that people of faith could be members of an authentic community where each member depended on the other, where each member cared for the other, where each member could live out the command of love of neighbor. What a precious act of love it is to pray for one another.

At the heart of this communion is the reality that relationships built on the foundation of grace are relationships that never end. Even death is not the end, nor is it a separation. Quite the contrary, death is simply the beginning of a new phase in eternal life, and in many ways a person who has died is closer to his or her loved ones than ever before. Just as a man or woman loved, cared for, and prayed for his or her loved ones on this earthly journey, they do the same in heaven, but in a much more powerful way. For the person who is in heaven is a person who dwells in the sphere of perfection and thus is a person who has been cleansed and purified of all his or her imperfections and sins (2 M 12:46f). The powerful prayers of the pure of heart cannot be denied.

Whether from earth or from heaven, we pray as a community of faith, as the Church.

Expressions of Prayer

Vocal Prayer

Vocal prayer is a form of prayer that lays the groundwork and nourishes all other forms of prayer. As vocal prayer progresses it opens our being for the higher forms of prayer.[88] Vocal prayer is the initial form of contemplative prayer.[89]

Vocal prayer is the incarnation of a person's heart's interaction with God. Words bring flesh to prayer. Human nature demands that our whole body participate in the worship of God —

---
[88] *Way*, Ch. 25.
[89] CCC 2702.

body, soul, and spirit. Prayer is the worship of God with our whole being (cf. Mt 11:25-26; Mk 14:36).

Meditation

> What is meditating on Christ? It is simply this, thinking habitually and constantly of Him and of His deeds and sufferings. It is to have Him before our minds as One whom we may [reflect upon], worship, and address when we rise up, when we lie down, when we eat and drink, when we are at home and abroad, when we are working, or walking, or at rest, when we are alone, and again when we are in company; this is meditating. And by this, and nothing short of this, will our hearts come to feel as they ought.[90]   *John Henry Newman*

For the Carthusian monk, Guigo II, "meditation is the busy application of the mind to seek with the help of one's own reason the knowledge of hidden truth."[91] Meditation in a most profound way moves a person away from unhealthy, "worldly" things.[92]

Meditation is the seeking of the life of God. The mind seeks to search out the mystery of life in meditation. Through Sacred Scripture, Sacred Tradition, spiritual books, sacred icons, liturgical texts and seasons as well as through history and creation we encounter many answers to the mystery of life. We also encounter the path that we must travel.

Meditation enables a person to encounter his or her deepest self. The book of life is opened to be explored. In this exploration

---

[90] John Henry Newman, *Parochial and Plain Sermons* (London: Longmans, Green, and Co., 1910) VI, 41.
[91] *Guigo II: The Ladder of Monks: A Letter on the Contemplative Life and Twelve Meditations*, trans. Edmund College, O.S.B., and James Walsh, S.J. (Kalamazoo: Cistercian Publications, 1981), 68.
[92] *Living Flame*, St. 3, no. 32; *Ascent*, Bk. III, Ch. 15, no. 2.

we ask: "Lord, what do you want me to do?" Meditation helps us to be well grounded in the life of Christ (cf. Mk 4:4-7; 15-19).

Meditation eventually will transform itself into contemplation, the only means for complete union with God.[93] As the *Catechism* states:

> Meditation engages thought, imagination, emotion, and desire. This mobilization of faculties is necessary in order to deepen our convictions of faith, prompt the conversion of our heart, and strengthen our will to follow Christ. Christian prayer tries above all to meditate on the mysteries of Christ, as in the *lectio divina* or the rosary. This form of prayerful reflection is of a great value, but Christian prayer should go further: to the knowledge of the love of the Lord Jesus, to union with him.[94]

Contemplative Prayer

> Contemplative prayer in my opinion is nothing else than a close sharing between friends; it means taking time frequently to be alone with him who we know loves us.[95]
>
> *St. Teresa of Avila*

Contemplation is the quest for the one "whom my soul loves" (Sg 1:7; cf. 3:1-4). We enter this form of prayer in quiet, poverty, and pureness of faith. We seek to be offered up to God in this experience; we ask to be purified and transformed into the image and likeness we were meant to be transformed into; that is, in the image and likeness of Jesus Christ. Contemplation is love welcoming love (cf. Lk 7:36-50; 19:1-10). It is victory through total surrendering. In contemplation the "Father strengthens our in-

---

[93] *Ascent*, Bk. II, Ch. 16, no. 7.
[94] CCC 2708.
[95] *Life*, 8, 5.

ner being with power through his Spirit so 'that Christ may dwell in [our] hearts through faith' and we may be 'grounded in love'" (Eph 3:16-17).[96]

Contemplation is the entrance into the sphere of the experience of God which transcends the limits of anything we hear, see, touch, smell, imagine, etc. It is beyond the limits of the internal and external senses. The God who transcends all speaks in silence to the heart of the person engaged in contemplation. He speaks with a presence of such intensity that the senses are incapable of grasping the fullness of this presence.

Aspects of Prayer

Blessing

Blessing exemplifies the basic movement of prayer. When we pray, we pray in an ascending order. We pray in the power of the Holy Spirit, through the Son, to the Father. In such a fashion we can be said to be blessing God who is the source of all blessings (cf. Eph 1:3-14; 2 Cor 1:3-7; 1 P 1:3-9). Through the grace of the Holy Spirit that descends through the Son and from the Father we are in turn blessed from the source of all blessings (cf. 2 Cor 13:14; Rm 15:5-6; Eph 6:23-24). Because "God blesses, the human heart can in return bless the One who is the source of every blessing."[97]

Adoration

Adoration is an act of humility, the doorway to holiness. In an act of adoration a person makes himself or herself aware that he or she is a created being in the presence of an almighty, omni-

---
[96] CCC 2714.
[97] CCC 2626.

Foundational Points

scient Creator (cf. Ps 95:1-6). Adoration is the realization that we have been saved by a Savior, by the King of all kings. It is the recognition that we have been set free from the slavery of sin to be a child of God (cf. Ps 24:9-10).

Petition

Through our petitions to God we are making present, in the most obvious of ways, the reality that we are in a relationship with God. In the act of asking, beseeching, pleading, invoking, entreating, and crying out to God we show our need and love for God (cf. Rm 15:30; Col 4:12). A petition is an acknowledgment that one is a sinner in need of a savior. It is an act of turning toward God (cf. Rm 8:22-24, 26). Prayers of petition require the awareness that one is in need of forgiveness (cf. Lk 18:13) and that one is in need of the gifts of humility and trust (cf. 1 Jn 1:7-2:2; 3:22).

Intercessions

An intercessory prayer is a unique form of a prayer of petition. It is closely modeled on Jesus' prayers. While it is true that Jesus is the one intercessor (cf. Rm 8:34; 1 Jn 2:1; 1 Tm 2:5-8; Heb 7:25), Jesus has granted the gift to all in grace to intercede in him, with him, and through him (cf. Lk 23:28, 34; Rm 8:26-27; 10:1; 12:14; Ac 7:60; 12:5; 20:36; 21:5; Eph 6:18-20; 2 Cor 9:14; Ph 1:3-4; 2:4; 1 Th 5:25; 2 Th 1:11; Col 1:3; 4:3-4; 1 Tm 2:1). A person of faith is a member of a community of love, the Church, the Body, the Bride of Christ (cf. Col 1:24; 2 Cor 11:2). As a consequence each member is to help the other members. Each member is called to love the other members. But God demands even more; he calls us to love even those who are outside the boundaries of the mystical Body. We must also pray for persecutors and all enemies of the Gospel (cf. Lk 6:35).

Thanksgiving

We give thanks to God for being freed from sin and slavery. We give thanks for the gift of grace, the gift of eternal life with God. We give thanks for being made a *new creation* in Christ (cf. 2 Cor 5:17). Because of the precious gift of immortality, because of all God's precious gifts, every event in our life, even the most difficult, the most painful, is worthy of thanksgiving. As St. Paul states: "Give thanks in all circumstances; for this is the will of God in Christ Jesus for you" (1 Th 5:18). In the mystery that is life, even the most hideous of circumstances can be transformed into a gift. Within the mystery of suffering is the mystery of love, and within the mystery of love is the mystery of suffering.

Praise

When we praise God we are worshipping God for simply being God. We are not focused on God's gifts, his "goodies," but simply on God. We praise God because *HE IS*! It is the prayer of the pure of heart and consequently it is the prayer that embraces all other prayers (cf. Rm 8:16; 16:25-27; 1 Cor 8:6; Ac 2:47; 3:9; 4:21; 13:48; Eph 1:3-14, 20-21; 5:14, 19; Col 1:15-20; 3:16; Ph 2:6-11; 1 Tm 3:16; 6:15-16; 2 Tm 2:11-13; Jude 24-25; Jm 1:17; Rv 4:8-11; 5:9-14; 6:10; 7:10-12).

The Battle of Prayer

Prayer is a gift that requires grace. Prayer is always brought about by an act of God. Our part in the experience of prayer is to respond to this initiative. We must remember that even before we can cry out to God, God is already there initiating that cry.

Prayer is a battle because it is a struggle against the consequences of original sin, concupiscence, and the temptations of the devil. Time constraints, the inability to experience or understand the supernatural, a preoccupation with sensuality, the sense that prayer is an escape rather than an encounter, the sense of discouragement, dryness, wounded pride, sin, and so forth all have an impact on our ability to pray. What is required of from us is a response, in grace, to the battle with the armaments of humility, trust, and perseverance.[98]

The battle in prayer is extremely important for our spiritual growth, for the wounds of the battle help us discern where we are on this spiritual road. We are able to see if we are closer to victory or defeat by observing our wounds. For example, distractions in prayer help us to see what we are attached to, which master we serve (cf. Mt 6:21, 24). Are we vigilant in the battle or have we become lax (cf. Mt 26:41)? Dryness in prayer can tell us whether we are being asked to walk by faith or if we are being asked to repent and turn back to God; in other words, is the dryness due to progress in holiness or is it due to sinfulness? Does distress help us to trust more or does it lead to despair (cf. Rm 5:3-5)? Prayers that seem not to be answered can clarify our motives in prayer: Do we love God as an instrument of selfishness or as a God who deserves love for simply being God?

In humility, trust and perseverance all prayers are heard, yet not all prayers are answered the way we want them to be answered. Prayers are always answered in a manner that is best for the eternal destiny of the petitioner (cf. Mt 6:8; Jm 4:1-10; 1:5-8; 5:16). We may pray to win the lottery on a Monday and yet not win. Does that mean God did not answer the prayer? Quite the contrary, God did answer the prayer: He said you don't need the money from the lottery, at least at this moment! The prayer was answered but not in the way we had hoped. If our prayers are

---

[98] CCC 2726-2728.

united to the Christ who prays in us, with us, and for us, then we will obtain what we desire (cf. Heb 5:7; 7:25; 9:24).[99]

The sense of unanswered prayers can often lead to the abandonment of the spiritual life for the selfish of heart. Thus, the love-driven gifts of humility and trust are so important for they empower the love-driven gift of perseverance that is essential for any battle (cf. 1 Th 5:17; Eph 5:20; 6:8).

Victory leads to enlightenment, peace and happiness. Defeat leads to slavery (cf. Gal 5:16-25).

Sacraments

For the Catholic, sacraments are efficacious and therefore essential for growth in holiness. Sacraments produce what they signify. A sacrament imparts grace to the individual (Ac 2:38; 8:17; 19:4-7; 1 P 3:19-22).[100] Thus, a person's disposition on receiving the sacraments has a great impact on his or her holiness.[101]

Baptism[102]

> Baptism regenerates us in the life of the Son of God; unites us to Christ and to His Body, the Church; it anoints us in the Holy Spirit, making us spiritual temples.[103]
>
> *Pope John Paul II*

Baptism is a sacrament with real power and it is a sacrament that is necessary for salvation, for it is by baptism that we are "born

---

[99] CCC 2735-2742.
[100] Cf. CCC 1076-1130; 1210-1211.
[101] Cf. ST IIIa, q. 89, a. 2.
[102] Cf. CCC 1213-1274.
[103] John Paul II, *Celebrate 2000: Reflections on Jesus, the Holy Spirit, and the Father* (Ann Arbor: Servant Publications, 1996), 40.

again" of *water* and the *Spirit* (Jn 3:5; Mk 16:16). In baptism we enter into Christ's death and resurrection (cf. Rm 6:3-4). We put on Christ in baptism (Gal 3:27). Baptism cleanses us from original sin, personal sin, and the punishment for sin (Mk 16:16; Jn 3:5; Ac 2:38f; 22:16; Rm 6:3-6; Gal 3:7; 1 Cor 6:11; Eph 5:26; Col 2:12-14; Heb 10:22). We become a new creation in Christ and a partaker in the divine nature (2 P 1:4). We become a member of the Church as an adopted child of God (cf. 1 Cor 12-13; 27). We becomes a Temple of the Holy Spirit (Ac 2:38; 19:5f) with an indelible mark or character on our soul which enables us to share in the priesthood of Christ and in his passion (Mk 10:38f; Lk 12:50).

Confirmation[104]

Confirmation perfects baptismal grace. Once confirmed we are strengthened by the Holy Spirit to be a powerful witness of Christ's self-communicating love to the world. We become a strengthened member in the mission of the Church, the proclamation of the Gospel. Like baptism, a sacred mark or seal is imprinted on the soul, forever changing it. In receiving this sacrament by a bishop or a delegated priest, we are making a commitment to profess the faith and to serve the world in word and deed as disciples of Christ (Ac 19:5-6; 8:16-17; Heb 6:1-2; 2 Cor 1:21-22; Eph 1:13).

The Eucharist[105]

St. Justin Martyr, in the year 150 AD, some fifty years after the death of the last apostle John, writes to the Emperor Anto-

---

[104] Cf. CCC 1285-1314.
[105] Cf. CCC 1322-1405.

ninus Pius regarding the long-standing practice of early Christian worship:

> On the day we call the day of the sun, all who dwell in the city or country gather in the same place.
> The memoirs of the apostles and the writings of the prophets are read, as much as time permits.
> When the reader has finished, he who presides over those gathered admonishes and challenges them to imitate these beautiful things.
> Then we all rise together and offer prayers for ourselves… and for all others, wherever they may be, so that we may be found righteous by our life and actions, and faithful to the commandments, so as to obtain eternal salvation.
> When the prayers are concluded we exchange the kiss. Then someone brings bread and a cup of water and wine mixed together to him who presides over the brethren.
> He takes them and offers praise and glory to the Father of the universe, through the name of the Son and of the Holy Spirit and for a considerable time he gives thanks (in Greek: *eucharistian*) that we have been judged worthy of these gifts.
> When he has concluded the prayers and thanksgiving, all present give voice by an acclamation by saying: 'Amen.'
> When he who presides has given thanks and the people have responded, those whom we call deacons give to those present the "eucharisted" bread, wine, and water and take them to those who are absent.[106]

In explaining the mystery indicated by the word "eucharisted," Justin states:

---

[106] St. Justin Martyr, *First Apology*, 65-67; PG 6, 428-429.

Foundational Points

> We call this food Eucharist… since Jesus Christ our Savior was made incarnate by the word of God and had both flesh and blood for our salvation, so too, as we have been taught, the food which has been made into the Eucharist by the Eucharistic prayer set down by Him, and by the change of which our blood and flesh is nourished, is both the flesh and the blood of that incarnated Jesus.[107]

It is a wonder how little things change in 2000 years!

The Eucharist is the "source and summit of our faith." All things flow from the Eucharist and return back to it.

The sacrifice of the Mass is prefigured in Genesis 14:18; 22:13, foretold in Malachi 1:10f., and attested to in 1 Corinthians 10:16, 18-21; 11:23-26 and Hebrews 13:10. It is the real presence of Christ, his real body and blood (Mt 26:26-28; Mk 14:22-24; Lk 22:19f; Jn 6:51f; 1 Cor 10:16; 11:24f).

The Mass is the *re-presenting*, or making present of what took place once and for all at Calvary (Heb 7:27; 9:12, 25-28; 10:10-14). Just as the Passover meal made present to those who participated in it the Exodus events, the Mass in a fuller way makes present what happened at Calvary. At every Mass, Calvary is made present to all. Mass is a participation in that one and only sacrifice on the cross at Calvary (cf. Heb 7:27).

It is the "source and summit of our faith," "the medicine of immortality, the antidote that we should not die, but live in Jesus forever."[108] The Eucharist increases a person's union with the Lord, forgives venial sins, and preserves that person from grave sin. By the fact that it strengthens the individual, it consequently strengthens the unity of the Church as Christ's mystical Body.

---

[107] St. Justin Martyr, *First Apology*, 66, quoted in William Jurgens, *The Faith of the Early Fathers*, vol. 1 (Collegeville: The Liturgical Press, 1970), 55.

[108] St. Ignatius of Antioch, *Ephesians*, 20, trans. Kirsopp Lake in *Apostolic Fathers* (Cambridge: Harvard University Press, 1998).

...and having received the Food that gives life immediately after the procession, I thought only of God and myself; and I beheld my soul, under the similitude of wax softened by the fire, impressed like a seal upon the bosom of the Lord....[109] *St Gertrude the Great*

Reconciliation / Penance[110]

The forgiveness of serious sin, or what we call mortal/deadly sin (1 Jn 5:17) requires the authority of the priest as an authoritative, power-filled representative of God and of the community. When we look at the Scriptures (Mt 16:19; 18:18; Jn 20:21-23) it becomes obvious that God entrusted his apostles with the gift of forgiving sins.

Jesus has an important reason for giving the world the Sacrament of Penance. When we sin we harm our relationship with God, with the community, and we do damage to our own being. That is because through sin we break the two commandments that God placed side by side, the love of God and the love of neighbor as oneself (Mt 22:37-40).

The spiritual effects of the Sacrament of Penance are beautifully summarized in the *Catechism of the Catholic Church* (1496):

- reconciliation with God by which the penitent recovers grace;
- reconciliation with the Church;
- remission of eternal punishment incurred by mortal sins;
- remission, at least in part, of temporal punishments resulting from sin;
- peace and serenity of conscience, and spiritual consolation;
- an increase of spiritual strength for the Christian battle.

---

[109] *The Life and Revelations of Saint Gertrude, Virgin and Abbess of the Order of St. Benedict*, trans. M.F.C. Cusak (Westminster: Christian Classics, 1983), 87f.
[110] Cf. CCC 1422-1470.

Foundational Points

St. Ignatius of Antioch (ca. 107), the disciple of John the apostle and friend of the apostles Peter and Paul, recognized the importance of the necessity of confession to a priest: "The Lord... forgives all who repent, if their repentance leads to the unity of God and the council of the bishop."[111]

Anointing of the Sick[112]

> Are any among you sick? Let him call for the [priests] of the church, and let them pray over him, anointing him with oil in the name of the Lord; and the prayer of faith will save the sick man, and the Lord will raise him up; and if he has committed sins, he will be forgiven (Jm 5:14-15).

This sacrament confers special grace on those suffering from illness or old age. It is a sacrament that can only be administered by a bishop or a priest. Its power is in the unifying of a person's sufferings with the Passion of Christ. It brings God's healing and loving presence upon the person. At times the healing is spiritual, at times it is emotional or physical, but what God brings about is what is best for a person's eternal destiny, his or her salvation. If a person is unable to receive the Sacrament of Penance it forgives the sins of the person (Mk 6:12-13; Jm 5:13-15).

Matrimony[113]

Christ elevated marriage to the level of a sacrament by the gift of grace. The reality of a man who gives himself completely, without doubt, without reservation, fully to his wife, and a wife who gives herself completely, without doubt, fully to her husband

---

[111] St. Ignatius of Antioch, *Philadelphians*, 8, trans. Lake.
[112] Cf. CCC 1499-1525.
[113] Cf. CCC 1601-1658.

can only come about by the supernatural gift of grace. It is only in this way that two can really become one (Mt 19:3-6; Mk 10:6-9). Because of this unity to which God calls a couple, marriage must be holy, indissoluble, and open to life (1 Th 4:4; 1 Tm 2:15). Marriage must mirror Christ's love for his own Bride, the Church (Eph 5:25, 32-32). It mirrors God's covenant with his people. Marriage is, therefore, that which must be blessed by the Church. Ignatius of Antioch, the disciple of the apostle John, in describing the elevation of marriage to a sacrament, states:

> It is right for men and women who marry to be united with the bishop's approval. In that way their marriage will follow God's will and not the promptings of lust.[114]

Holy Orders[115]

The Sacrament of Holy Orders is an indispensable part of the Church. Without it the Church would not be able to trace itself back to apostolic times, and therefore back to Christ.

The Church makes a distinction between the common priesthood of all the faithful (1 P 2:9) and the ordained priesthood. All Christians are called to be a priestly people, a healing, loving, forgiving people, but some of the faithful are specifically set aside by Jesus and the apostles for unique ministerial roles. The priesthood conferred by the Sacrament of Holy Orders is one that is specifically designated for teaching, leading worship, and meeting the pastoral needs of the people. Holy Orders confer an indelible spiritual mark on the soul.

The most important of the Holy Orders is that of the bishop because he serves as the visible head of the local or particular

---

[114] St. Ignatius, *Letter to Polycarp*, 5.
[115] Cf. CCC 1536-1600.

Church. Every bishop in the world can trace himself from one bishop to another bishop to another bishop all the way back in time to an apostle. Consequently, they have the fullness of the priesthood and are crucial in protecting the true faith. The greatest of the bishops is of course the Pope, since he is the successor of the leader of the apostles, Peter.

The next order is the presbyter or what we commonly call the priest. He is a "prudent coworker" and extension of the bishop. He receives his authority from the bishop, and teaches in power because of his tie to the tree of apostolic succession.

The final order is that of the deacon who likewise is attached to the bishop, but who is entrusted primarily with works of charity.

Holy Orders were instituted by Christ (Lk 22:19; Jn 20:22f), conferred by the imposition of hands by an apostle or his successor (Ac 6:6; 13:3; 14:23) and give grace (1 Tm 4:14; 2 Tm 1:6-7).

St. Clement of Rome, the friend of the apostles Peter and Paul, who in fact was ordained a bishop by Peter himself, eloquently teaches us about the gift of priesthood:

> The apostles preached to us the Gospel received from Jesus Christ, and Jesus Christ was God's Ambassador. Christ, in other words, comes with a message from God, and the apostles with a message from Christ. Both these orderly arrangements, therefore, originate from the will of God. And so, after receiving their instructions and being fully assured through the Resurrection of our Lord Jesus Christ, as well as confirmed in faith by the word of God, they went forth, equipped with the fullness of the Holy Spirit, to preach the good news that the Kingdom of God was close at hand. From land to land, accordingly, and from city to city they preached, and from among their earliest converts appointed men whom they had tested by the Spirit to act as bishops and deacons for future believers. And this was

no innovation, for, a long time before the Scriptures had spoken about bishops and deacons; for somewhere it says: I will establish overseers in observance of the law and their ministers in fidelity.[116]

St. Clement continues:

Our apostles, too, were given to understand by our Lord Jesus Christ that the office of bishop would give rise to intrigues. For this reason, equipped as they were with perfect foreknowledge, they appointed the men mentioned before, and afterwards laid down a rule once for all to this effect: when these men die, other approved men shall succeed to their sacred ministry.... Happy the presbyters [priests] who have before now completed life's journey and taken their departure in mature age and laden with fruit![117]

In Conclusion

In order to grasp the nature of the spiritual journey, we need to grasp the foundational aspects that propel this journey. As we proceed to the traditional stages of the spiritual journey it will be essential to keep in mind what has been discussed in this foundational chapter.

---

[116] St. Clement of Rome, *Epistle to the Corinthians*, 42, quoted in *The Companion to the Catechism* (San Francisco: Ignatius Press, 1995), 376.

[117] Ibid., 44, quoted in *Companion*, 377.

3

The Purgative Stage
The Age of the Superficial

> May the Lord Jesus touch our eyes, as he did those of the blind. Then we shall begin to see in visible things those which are invisible. May he open our eyes to gaze, not on present realities, but on the blessings to come. May he open the eyes of our heart to contemplate God in Spirit, through Jesus Christ the Lord, to whom belong power and glory through all eternity.
> *Origen*

The Pillars of Holiness

Humility

> Humility is the first entry into religion, as it was Christ's first step into the world.... Humility has always been the cornerstone to sanctity....[118]
> *Francisco de Osuna*

Humility is the doorway to holiness, for it is the doorway to true self-knowledge. It is important to realize that humility is not

---

[118] *Francisco de Osuna: The Third Spiritual Alphabet*, trans. and intro. Mary E. Giles (Mahwah: Paulist Press, 1981), 494f.

low self-esteem, rather it is the recognition that all of our gifts are from God. Humility is just another name for self-knowledge — that ability to know ourselves the way God truly knows us. Humility avoids unnecessary and unworthy praise, self-seeking, the impressing of others or boasting, and the pursuit of worldly "things" such as fame. Humility promotes the awareness of the need for growth through the recognition of our weaknesses and sins. It acknowledges the need for compassion, assistance and strength. It promotes a clear conscience and the strength to bear the cross. It rejoices in being corrected and sees reproaches as kisses from God. Humility helps us to be a person for others and recognizes that all things and activities are to be for the glory and honor of God, and that all of life is part of God's providential plan.[119]

Love[120]

God is love and whoever does not know love does not know God (cf. 1 Jn 4:7). The guiding force of grace is love, for we always move toward what we love. Without love, outward deeds are of little significance. On the other hand, to love much is to authentically do much. Love makes us pure of heart: it makes what we appear outwardly the reality of what we are inwardly. In love all is done for the honor and glory of God. Love makes us seek to turn all things to good. Love never seeks to justify or rationalize the evil we have done. Love makes us never long for special attention or affection to the exclusion of others. In love we recognizes the inseparable nature of the love of God and the love of neighbor. Any authentic love of God requires an authentic love of neighbor and any authentic love of neighbor requires an au-

---

[119] Thomas à Kempis, *Imitation of Christ*, Bk. I, 2, 3, 7; Bk. II, 2, 4, 5, 12; Bk. III, 17, 20, 22, 24, 29, 35-36, 46, 50, 54.
[120] *Imitation of Christ*, Bk. I, 15, 19, 24; Bk. II, 3, 5, 8; Bk. III, 35.

thentic love of God. Love makes us acknowledge that if we seek forgiveness we must be forgiving. Love makes us look at the best in others. It is not suspicious of anyone.

> Love is patient and kind; love is not jealous or boastful; it is not arrogant or rude. Love does not insist on its own way; it is not irritable or resentful; it does not rejoice at wrong, but rejoices in the right. Love bears all things, believes all things, hopes all things, endures all things. Love never ends (1 Cor 13:4-8).

Silence

The spiritual journey requires an openness to silence, to calm (cf. Ps 62:1). Silence allows us to be open to God's will and therefore is a must in our spiritual journey. Silence allows us to read, reflect, meditate, and pray in an authentic manner. It allows us to spend time with God and learn from him. A person who talks too much is a person who knows too little. Silence permits growth in intimacy with God, for God speaks in the silence. Silence affords the opportunity for us to be prepared for work, for proclaiming the Gospel to the ends of the world. Silence helps us to act prudently in our work. It promotes sincere repentance and contrition. It promotes the recognition of our sinfulness and allows us to search the depths of our conscience. Silence promotes humility, love, mortification, and the seeking of truth. It recognizes the emptiness of "worldly" things. It allows us to experience peace of mind and to rest in the Lord. It keeps us focused on death, on our eternal destiny, on our purpose and meaning in life.[121]

---

[121] *Imitation of Christ*, Bk. I, 24-25.

Hunger for Truth

God is truth, and since he is truth, the spiritual path must be a quest for truth (cf. Jn 4:24). Truth helps us seek to follow right reason and an informed conscience. It aids us to affirm the imperfections of human knowledge and thus the need for the correcting power of divine revelation. The hunger for truth helps us seek the advice of holy and learned people, and the advice of the saints and the Fathers of the Church. Truth grants us the gift of thinking about what is being said and not about who is saying it. We become cautious in what is being portrayed as truth. We sift and distinguish the good from the evil. The hunger for truth helps us experience life in authentic freedom. Often the devil makes what is evil seem very appealing in order to enslave us. The hunger for truth helps us to seek beyond what we experience through the senses. Truth opens the heart and guides us to discover the God who is within and helps us to seek all that is necessary for salvation.[122]

Mortification and Detachment

> Love is a good disposition of the soul by which one prefers no being to the [experience] of God. It is impossible to reach the habit of this love if one has any attachments to earthly things.[123]   *St. Maximus Confessor*

> Jesus has many lovers of his heavenly kingdom, but few cross-bearers.[124]   *Thomas à Kempis*

---

[122] *Imitation of Christ*, Bk. I, 2, 5; Bk. II, 45; Bk. III 4, 50.
[123] *Maximus Confessor: Selected Writings*, trans. George C. Berthold (Mahwah: Paulist Press, 1985), n. 1.
[124] *Imitation of Christ*, Bk. II, Ch. 11.

> If God in His love for the human race had not given us tears, those being saved would be few indeed and hard to find....[125] Tears come from nature, from God, from suffering good and bad, from vainglory, from licentiousness, from love, from the remembrance of death, and from numerous other causes.... Tears can wash away sins as water washes away something written. And as some, lacking water, use other means to wipe off what is written, souls lacking tears beat and scour away their sins with grief, groans, and deep sorrow....[126]
>
> St. John Climacus

Our passions, affections, or feelings can help us in seeking the good and avoiding the evil. Among the primary passions that affect us are love, hatred, fear, joy, sadness, and anger. In and of themselves, feelings, affections, or emotions are neither good nor evil. They are neutral. It is what we do with these passions that can cause spiritual harm. In other words, if the feeling of love is picked up by the virtue of justice, we are likely to be merciful in the carrying out of justice. If, however, the feeling of love is picked up by a vice, such as lust, then authentic love becomes perverted. If the passions are in order with right reason and good will, then they are beneficial in the spiritual life, particularly in the early purgative stages. If these passions, however, are contrary to right reason and the proper use of the will, then they are the source of self-destruction and slavery (cf. Jn 8:34).[127]

Detachment involves a healthy indifference to worldly concerns. By being detached of all we can love all authentically, the way God intended all to be loved. We seek to be detached of all that is not for the glory and honor of God; on the other hand, *we*

---

[125] *John Climacus: The Ladder of Divine Ascent*, trans. Colm Luibheid and Norman V. Russell (Mahwah: Paulist Press, 1982), 137.
[126] Ibid., 139-140, 259.
[127] St. Augustine, *De civ. Dei*, 14, 7, 2: PL 41, 410; ST Ia IIae, q. 24, a.1, 3.

are called to be attached to all that is for the glory and honor of God. Mortification involves the denial of the passions and appetites in order to purify them and in order to purify our direction toward God. Detachment and mortification are both essential aspects of the spiritual life for they help us to empty the self of all that is not of God. They are lessons in self-mastery, which is at the heart of holiness and happiness.

We are called through detachment and mortification to lead a life of obedience, self-discipline and simplicity. We are called to avoid vanity and pride and the propensity for lying and gossiping, which are signs of self-infatuation. We must be aware of deceptive and inordinate pleasures which are momentary, but that in the long run lead to sadness and remorse. We must seek the best in people and fight off the innate inclination to see the worst in them. We must seek to uncover in others the image of Christ to love, and we must seek to model our life after Christ's. We must avoid trying to see ourselves as always better than others. We must be able to realize that others are often better in many ways. We must avoid criticizing and judging others, for people are so often mistaken in their assessments of others and therefore offend God. We often judge according to our emotions and our self-will and stubbornness. We often judge with poorly formed, self-seeking opinions. Bearing the defects of others in patience and praying for their holiness is precious. It is so easy to fall into the trap of seeking perfection in others but refusing to see the imperfections in our very nature.

We must seek the submission of our will to God's by being faithful to Scripture, Sacred Tradition, and the teachings of the Church and its authoritative leadership. We must seek to conform our will to God's and not the other way around. We must do, at times, what we do not want to do and to leave undone what we would like to do. We are called to rejoice in adversity, in not having our way. Not having our way purifies us to put our hope in God and not in "worldly" things.

We must seek devout conversations and delve into all aspects of the spiritual life. We must, consequently, avoid "worldly" people for they lead us into dangerous waters.

We must resist temptation by turning to God immediately. By doing so we become humble, clean, and learned. However, given the reality of unavoidable temptations, we must take the opportunity to grow through times of temptation. Our response to temptation shows who we truly are.

We must continually seek to repent and experience sorrow for sin. We must keep our eye continually on death by acts of meditation. We are called to embrace suffering as a precious gift that purifies us of all that is not of God. We must pray that we do not find too much consolation, for too much consolation can lead to sins of presumption and pride. We must unite our sufferings to Christ's patiently, willingly, and without complaint. We must not seek so much rest as patience and endurance on this earthly journey.

All things and all works must be directed toward God for happiness. Anything not directed toward God is earthbound and ultimately a disappointment. We must find comfort in the reality that from all eternity God knew the path we would take and that God would always be there to meet our deepest needs. We must remember that all "things" are part of God's providential plan. Nothing happens by chance.[128]

---

[128] *Imitation of Christ*, Bk. I, 3-14; 16; 20-23; Bk. II, 2, 10; Bk. III, 9, 13, 15, 19, 20, 22, 24, 31, 35, 37-39, 46-50, 54.

LIGHT, HAPPINESS AND PEACE

Surrender and Trust

> Total abandonment consists of giving oneself fully to God because God has given himself to us. If God, who owes us nothing, is willing to give us nothing less than himself, can we respond by giving him only a part of ourselves? …Jesus wants us to put all our trust in him. We have to renounce our desires in order to work for our own perfection. Even if we feel like a boat without a compass on the high seas, we are to commit ourselves fully to him, without trying to control his actions.
>
> I cannot long for a clear perception of my progress along the route, nor long to know precisely where I am on the path of holiness. I ask Jesus to make me a saint. I leave it to him to choose the means that can lead me in that direction.[129]
>
> *Mother Teresa*

Life is an adventure in which God is in control. God's providential will cannot be thwarted. Any attempt at thwarting God's will always lead to disappointments, anxieties, and every other kind of unhappiness one can imagine. Only in God's will is there rest (Ps 62:2). Only in God's will is there peace and happiness.

The key to life is surrendering to God's will and trusting that he will take us to that place which is best for our soul. Life must be experienced as an adventure: Every morning we must wake up and say: "Lord, what adventure do you have planned for me today? Will it be a joyous one or will it be a hard and difficult one? In any case, I'm ready for the adventure and I joyously take it on, for I know you are in control and that you will never abandon me! I surrender and I trust, for in surrendering and trusting I find the victory of my life."

Surrendering and trusting in God is a lifelong process, but

---

[129] Mother Teresa, *Heart of Joy*, 125-126.

Predominant Inclinations and Faults

All of us have a predominant fault or faults (cf. 2 Cor 12:7). A predominant fault is a weakness that we bear as a consequence of our natural temperament (or as a consequence of the development of a pathological disorder). Predominant flaws tend to be most troubling to the spiritual journey. It has a powerful effect on our feelings, judging, willing, acting, and so forth. It can at times be hidden and at times disguised as a virtue (e.g., poor self-esteem as humility). It can at times be sinless or at times be the source of a great many sins.

In the purgative stage of spirituality there is the beginning of a process of enlightenment: the old self is coming into conflict with the new self. The old way of life is now being replaced with a new way of life, a way that is happier and more productive. This *new self* becomes more and more new and healthy as it discards all that is negative in the old self and keeps all that is positive of the old self. Christ, the *Great Physician* (cf. Mk 2:17), is beginning to open our eyes in ways that they were never open before. Our life is beginning to be enlightened in ways never before experienced and God is now challenging us to change for the better. This revolutionary process, which begins the purgative stage, will grow to its ultimate fruition through the illuminative stage and into the unitive stage.[130]

It is important that in discussing the above predominate inclinations and faults, that we remember that in the spiritual per-

---

[130] Part of the enlightenment process may be the awareness that we are in need of psychological or psychiatric help.

son all of the theological virtues, the cardinal and capital virtues, and all the gifts of the Spirit are active. It is simply that some are more obviously active than others. Furthermore, as one progresses in the spiritual journey, the gifts and virtues become less and less hampered by the taint of sin and thus the fruits of the life of grace, such as charity, joy, peace, patience, benignity, goodness, longanimity, mildness, faith, modesty, continency, and chastity, flow more profusely and significantly.

The following are some of the most troubling wounds found in the purgative stage:

Alienation

> There are many kinds of poverty. Even in countries where the economic situation seems to be a good one, there are expressions of poverty hidden in a deep place, such as the tremendous loneliness of people who have been abandoned and who are suffering.
> As far as I am concerned, the greatest suffering is to feel alone, unwanted, unloved.
> The greatest suffering is also having no one, forgetting what an intimate, truly human relationship is, not knowing what it means to be loved....[131]   *Mother Teresa*

Alienation is a symptom of modern society. The modern world can at times be a very cut-throat world. People are often made to feel replaceable, small, powerless, unsupported, unrecognized, overwhelmed, confused, and disassociated with others, including family. Such a world leads people to often feel they do not belong, that life is meaningless, valueless, that they have no

---

[131] Mother Teresa, *In My Own Words: Special Memorial Edition* (Liguori: Liguori Publications, 1996), 91.

role in life. They can become self-absorbed, cold, joyless, depressed, bored, and emotionally numb or distant. They are often people whose self-image or self-esteem is terribly damaged.

In the purgative stage there is the beginning of the awareness that we are created in the "image and likeness" of God, that we are precious to God for simply being a person. Our dignity and mission as an adopted child of God, as a co-heir to the divine mysteries, as a participant in the divine life all start to make us find a sense of meaning and purpose, a unique sense of direction that is grace-induced. It is a time where we move from self-centeredness to other-centeredness. We become a person for others. A hardened, defensive heart becomes replaced by an open, gentle heart — a heart that is surrendered to the will of God, whatever it may be. Life, with its trials and tribulations, becomes an adventure. "Wherever you take me Lord, I'm ready for the ride!"

Anger

Of all the crosses that Christians have to deal with, the cross of anger is the one that is the cause of more pain in the life of Christians than can ever be imagined.

Anger is a state marked by emotional agitations, particularly resentment, exasperation, indignation, impatience, egoism, aggressiveness, verbal and physical abuse, and even rage. Anger can be expressed in a manifest manner in which we are aware of the anger, or it may be manifested in a repressed or unconscious manner, in which we are unaware of it. Often this unconscious, repressed, or latent anger finds expression in depression, anxiety, and pathological disorders such as social anxiety disorder.

Very often, anger is rooted in an unconscious fear or emotional insecurity or anxiety which becomes repressed and surfaces as anger. Some anger is caused by more mundane reasons such as frustration which is associated with failing to attain one's goal in life, or the frustration which is associated with unpleasant trials and tribulations in life.

In the purgative stage, anger is the cross of crosses. As we progress in the purgative stage and into the higher stages of the spiritual life, anger is transformed more and more into a peaceful existence. The infused capital virtue of humility (which is another word for self-knowledge), the infused cardinal virtues of patience, justice, and courage, the theological virtue of charity (or love), and the Spirit's gifts of fortitude, understanding, and wisdom are the predominant forces that help to curb and heal anger.

Humility is the ability to recognize ourselves as we truly are. Grace, as we grow in response to it, helps us to see the deepest, most hidden aspects of our being. We grow to see repressed anxieties or pathologies that need healing, whether they are the product of our upbringing or a genetic predisposition. Patience and the gift of understanding allow us to pause and assess the situation before reacting to it. We recognize, little by little, the grudges, the unresolved issues, the distortion of facts (where we unreasonably view ourselves as the butt of all attacks), and the rationalization of our unjustified anger. The theological virtue of charity gives us a sense of *give and take* in relationships, a sense that we do not always have to win or have our own way. Self-centeredness gives way, little by little, to other-centeredness. The charitable person is able to direct his or her anger-producing forces into positive ends such as good works. The infused virtue of courage and the gift of courage also offer the opportunity for directing the anger-producing forces into more productive expressions, such as the gentle confrontation of injustices. Finally, the Spirit's gift of wisdom helps to put all of life's difficulties into their proper perspective; that is, all things are in one way or another part of God's divine providence. God is in control! Fear not!

Anxiety

Anxiety is an emotional state that makes us overly worried about the circumstances of life, thereby affecting our thinking, behaving, and feeling, indeed our entire being. We have, in the words of the philosopher Soren Kierkegaard, a "built-in" sense of anxiety about life in regard to illness, accidents, death, and so forth. This causes uneasiness, edginess, fatigue, attention deficits, and a preoccupation with things other than the task at hand. It can be at the conscious level or unconscious level of a person's personality. The key causes of this anxiety are found in repressed feelings and irrational or disproportionate fears over life's circumstances.

In the purgative stage anxiety is at its highest level and happiness is at its lowest. As we progress through the successive stages of the spiritual journey, anxiety begins to diminish and happiness begins to predominate.

As we progress in the spiritual life, the Spirit's gift of understanding as well as the active and infused virtue of humility helps us to discover the conscious and unconscious sources of anxiety. We become more aware of the sources of anxiety by a careful reflection on our experiences, such as our dreams, fantasies, thoughts, Freudian slips, etc. We become able to recognize our subconscious feelings and we are able to identify our irrational thoughts. Through the gift of counsel, and the corresponding virtue of humility, we can recognize the need for help, and the desire and courage to seek out this help and make changes that foster spiritual and physical integration. The virtue of temperance helps to moderate irrational thoughts and feelings. The gifts of wisdom, knowledge and piety help to calm our anxieties through journaling and meditation.

The theological virtue of hope and the gifts of wisdom, knowledge and understanding help to bring peace by enabling us to acknowledge that all things will be all right, for all things are in God's providential hands.

Meaninglessness in Life and Boredom

Meaninglessness makes a person prone to suicide, promiscuous behavior, addictions, and many other forms of self-destructive life choices. Without a sense of purpose and meaning we can easily find ourselves tottering on the verge of despair. We can become persons incapable of authentic love.

This sense of emptiness that is so often found in people today is caused by an inability to see the God who is at the very core of one's being, seeking a response to his self-communicating love.

This sense of meaninglessness often leads to the condition of boredom. Boredom is a state of being characterized by a sense of discontent. Chronic boredom is a cause of great harm on our spiritual journey. Boredom often makes us uninterested in our marriage partner, children, parents, relatives, neighbors, and so forth. It is characterized also by fatigue, impatience, vanity, self-absorption, lack of commitment, and a general sense of meaninglessness. Often depression follows boredom, for boredom leaves a sense of emptiness inside.

Boredom is most often caused by a lack of direction in life, and at times by an over-abundance of "things." Boredom is quite frequently the cancer of the rich.

What can be done for this sense of meaninglessness and boredom? The evangelical counsel of poverty, the gifts of understanding, wisdom, piety, fear of the Lord, the theological virtues of faith, hope, and love, the virtues of humility, temperance, and justice are key aspects in overcoming boredom and a sense of emptiness in life, for they help us acknowledge that no amount of fame, honor, comfort, leisure, or whatever, can bring about a lasting sense of fulfillment. Worldly "things" can give a temporary happiness, or bliss, or even meaning, but in the end, and with time, this happiness and sense of meaning disappears.

As we progress in the spiritual life we enter the sphere of

The Purgative Stage

meaningfulness, of fulfillment. We approach life filled with a sense of wonder and awe. Life, with its joys, trials and tribulations, becomes an adventure. Zeal becomes part of the life of God-infused persons who find meaning in living in God and loving God and neighbor. They seek the kingdom and the building of the kingdom. The virtue of justice moves them to be active in the world; the virtue of humility gives them the sense of identity as a child of God and moves them away from vanity; and the virtue of temperance helps them move away from self-absorption.

At the core of meaninglessness and boredom is a conscious or subconscious lack of belief or trust in God. Thus, prayer, reflection, and the fruits of the two works, are essential for authentic meaning. The great mathematician, philosopher, and theologian, Blaise Pascal, realized this sense of meaningfulness that could only be found in God in his famous "wager." It is to one's advantage, according to Pascal, to believe in God. In fact, to not believe in God is an absurdity and a sign of stupidity. If one believes in God one has a sense of meaning and purpose, goals, a feeling of happiness, peace, contentment, and light. Life is precious. If one is wrong and there is no God, then one has lived an enjoyable life and one has lost nothing at death. On the other hand, if one does not believe in God, then life is essentially meaningless. It is a life filled with emptiness, a life filled with chasing after temporary sparks of happiness that fizzle out. Such a life is a sad life, a life that dances with despair. If one were right, and there is no God, then one has lived a miserable life and has died miserably. If one is wrong in his or her disbelief in God, then one has lived a miserable life and one will have to pay the consequences for such a miserable, unbelieving life when faced with the face of meaning himself, God.

As we progress in the spiritual journey our vocation becomes very clear. It is a vocation to love. As St. Thérèse of Lisieux so beautifully put it:

Charity gave me the key to *my vocation*. I saw that if the Church was a body made up of different members, the most essential and important one of all would not be lacking; I saw that the Church must have *a heart*, that this heart must be on fire with love. I saw that it was love alone which moved her other members, and that were this love to fail, apostles would no longer spread the Gospel, and martyrs would refuse to shed their blood. I saw that all vocations are summed up in love and that love is all in all, embracing every time and place because it is eternal.

In a transport of ecstatic joy I cried: "Jesus, my Love, I have at last found my vocation; *it is love*! I have found my place in the Church's heart, the place You Yourself have given me, my God. Yes, there in the heart of Mother Church *I will be love*; so shall I be all things, so shall my dreams come true."[132]

For the spiritual there is always meaning!

Depression

Depression is an ailment that is characterized by brooding, fatigue, crying, and a lack of desire for life. As with many ailments, it can have a biological or genetic basis and therefore require an anti-depressant drug. It can be the product of repressed, bottled up anger or frustrations. It can be the consequence of an inability to find meaning in life and in death, and a sense of being helpless and alone in an overwhelming world. At times depression can be the product of the spiritual ailment of scrupulosity — distorted self-analysis and self-criticism.

The Spirit's gifts of understanding, knowledge, right judg-

---

[132] St. Thérèse of Lisieux, *The Story of a Soul*, trans. Michael Day (Rockford: TAN Books and Publishers, Inc., 1997), 199-200.

ment, and the virtues of courage and humility have a profound impact on helping us, if we should ever find ourselves in such a situation, recognize that we need help, whether psychiatric or psychological. Likewise the gifts and virtues help uncover and heal the wounds that accompany repressed, bottled up feelings and attitudes. They help bring to light the unresolved problems of life, particularly of childhood.

A sense of optimism and meaning in life, and the ability to overcome scrupulous feelings and thoughts is aided by the theological virtues of faith, hope, and love and the virtues of prudence and temperance. We begin to move away from a preoccupation with the self and move toward a preoccupation with the other. We no longer live in the pool or hole of self-absorption, but now live a life that can be characterized by being a person for others.

Spiritual journaling is very effective in coming in touch with our inner being, our inner-self.

Self-Destructiveness

The beginning of the spiritual journey is often marked with the recognition of many self-destructive tendencies, which are nourished by self-absorption and self-abasement. Such people totter on the edge of reality. The abuse of and addiction to alcohol, drugs, food, sex, and so forth, are the most common traits of the self-destructive person. With grace, God begins to enlighten those beset by these destructive forces to the need for healing and help.

The theological virtues of faith, hope, and love, the cardinal virtues of prudence, temperance, justice, and courage, the capital virtues of humility, generosity, mildness, etc., and the gifts of the Spirit, particularly the gifts of wisdom, understanding, knowledge, right judgment, reverence, and fear of the Lord (wonder and awe), all have a profound curative effect on the person with self-destructive tendencies.

They begin to seek out help and find healing in God's grace, which cures, elevates and builds upon a damaged nature. Egocentrism begins to be lost. The world is no longer seen as revolving around themselves. Self-hate and guilt are purified into an awareness of God's mercy and the need to accept God's mercy, his forgiving, loving touch. The need to punish others for whatever harm they may have caused is replaced with a desire to forgive and the need to pray for the holiness of the person or persons who caused the harm, and the realization that the person or persons who caused the harm need to be addressed in a gentle manner for the harm they have caused. The sense of meaninglessness and helplessness, particularly during times of anguish or illness, is overcome by the impetus of uniting one's meaning and suffering to that of the cross.

The loss of the sense of the cross in the world has been the cause of countless troubles in life.

Inability to Get Along with Others

The inability to get along with others is the source of many of the above problems and is the source of great pain. People who fail to get along with others often lack effective communication skills. They have frequent bouts of depression, emotional and physical isolation, distrust, and a "me against the world attitude." They often feel abused or used.

Such people have unrealistic expectations about life and are often prone to an overly idealistic vision of the world that leads them to become frustrated and angry over any type of disappointment. They often bear the scars of a low self-esteem. Such people are prone to become depressed and demoralized. They often have a tremendous need for recognition, to be thought of as important,

The Purgative Stage

to be loved. If they do not receive this recognition, they often misbehave in order to gain attention, even if the attention is a negative one. Anything is better than being ignored. Such people often like to play the role of victim or take on the opposite role of bully or dictator. Both roles are signs of low self-esteem. Such people often have an "eye for an eye" attitude. "You did this to me. Well, I'll do this to you!" "You called me insensitive; well, I call you stupid."

People with communication problems tend to send mixed signals, one verbal, the other psychological (e.g., a person on one level says he or she is truly interested in what another has to say, but that person's body language, such as crossed arms, more clearly says that he or she truly is not open to hearing anything). Such people are the ultimate gossipers and liars. They engage in gossip and lying for it helps them deal with their own low self-esteem. To rip into another brings a superficial sense of satisfaction to the person, for such a person can reason that "I am not so bad after all. Just look at that person!"

The Spirit's gifts of understanding, wisdom, and knowledge, right judgment and courage enable us to realize our weakness and need for help. With God's grace, we become aware, with or without professional help, of repressed realities in our life. The gift of understanding gives us a profound eye-opening experience regarding hidden messages and unrealistic expectations. We become aware of the truth about ourselves and about others. In humility, with the virtues of prudence and justice, we are able to see reality the way it authentically is and to act accordingly with integrity. The need for being a victim is overcome with the cardinal virtues of temperance, courage, justice, and prudence. The Spirit's gifts of wisdom, piety, and right judgment help us to see the divine spark in all human beings. For the bully, the capital virtues of humility, generosity, mildness, temperance, friendship, and the cardinal virtue of justice, and the theological virtues of love, of charity, and the Spirit's gift of reverence, help the person to value the dignity of others as created in the image and likeness of God. It also removes the obstacles that cause loneliness and isolation. The "eye for an eye" syndrome is eliminated by the virtues of love, prudence, temperance, justice, generosity, mildness, and the gifts of reverence and fear of the Lord. The person begins to see that what he or she does to another is being done to Christ.

Whether an individual suffers from an antisocial, schizotypal, avoidant, borderline, dependent, histrionic, narcissistic, obsessive-compulsive, paranoid, or schizoid personality disorder — or a combination of the above — he or she is not left without hope. Whether one suffers from excessive lying, gossiping, impulsivity, aggressiveness, irresponsibility, recklessness, suspiciousness, moodiness, anger, inflexibililty, rigidness, distrust, indifference, or egoism, there is hope. Whether one has a poor self-esteem or self-image, experiences an excessive fear of abandonment or loneliness, there is still hope. Whether one displays inappropriate social inhibitions, inappropriate emotional responses or lack of, whether one has an inability to experience remorse or sensitivity toward others, one has hope. Whether one shows signs of an inability to forgive, there is hope. Whether one bears the scars of hypersensitivity, clinging behavior, hunger for affection, attention seeking, or inappropriate fantasies and detachments, there is hope. Whether one gives signs of inappropriate entitlement or inappropriate idealism or perfection, there is hope. The life of holiness is the life that always directs one toward growth. In the power of grace, the enlightening, elevating, healing, and building structure of human life, there is always hope. For in grace, one is able to seek help, to grow, and to heal.

As we progress in the spiritual life we become open to God's call to holiness. Holiness implies "wholeness." Thus as we grow in the spiritual life, we grow to be psychologically, physically, and spiritually whole, for holiness is growth in the image and likeness of God, in the image and likeness of Christ. While complete "wholeness" or perfect holiness is impossible in this life, to the extent that we are able to grow in holiness, it is to that extent that we will grow in happiness, peace, contentment, and light.

The Blind Side

All people have a blind side. That is, a side to their personality that most people are able to spot, except for the person experiencing this blind spot. People can be egotistical, gossipers, compulsive manipulators and liars, vengeful, lacking self-esteem, etc., and not be in the least bit aware of these realities. Everyone around them, for the most part knows, but they themselves are completely oblivious to it. All people have various blind spots. The key to the spiritual life is being open to discovering these blind spots.

Blind spots are brought to light through all the gifts and virtues, but particularly the gifts of wisdom, understanding, and knowledge, and the capital virtue of humility. Through these gifts and in particular the infused gift of humility in combination with the gifts of the Spirit, we are able to see ourselves the way we truly are. Let us again remember that humility is just another word for self-knowledge. Hence, guided by these gifts we are able to reflect upon our actions and are able to make powerful examinations of conscience which enable us to see what we could not see before.

The gifts and virtues also enable us to reach out to others, particularly spiritual friends, who will in authentic love tell us what we may not want to hear regarding our character. True love can at times be very hurtful at first, but in the end, it is most precious. True love tells us what we need to hear, not what we want to hear!

Prayer in the Purgative Stage

Prayer in this initial stage of spirituality is primarily focused on prayers of petition. At this stage, we are still very much self-absorbed and thus are primarily concerned with getting "goodies" from God, as opposed to loving God for simply being God.

When praying for others there is often a secondary motive for the prayer which has an intended benefit for the petitioner. For example, we may pray for a brother going through a difficult time, with the intention that God will bring relief; however, mixed within this petition will often be the hope that God will take care of this brother during this difficult time because we are tired of having to be concerned for him and of having to support him. We can see that the prayer is not completely pure. It has a secondary motive.

Charismatic prayer is a very popular form of prayer in this early stage of spiritual development. Charismatic prayer, as emphasized in today's society, is that form of prayer that is marked with the charisms of the Holy Spirit — in particular the ability to speak in tongues, to interpret tongues, to prophesy, and to experience being "slain in the Spirit" (cf. 1 Cor 12:8-10). Charismatic prayer is most often associated with those in the purgative stage of spirituality since those in this stage tend to be intensely sense-oriented in their experiences of God. Hence, by its very nature, charismatic prayer is bound to give way to higher forms of prayer along the spiritual path. As we progress in the spiritual life, God does more of the communicating, and we do more of the listening. As we progress there is less noise and more silence. Charismatic prayer, as we progress, becomes more insight and discernment-oriented.

Prayer in the purgative stage — in the early stages of development — is quite simplistic and filled with many distractions. As St. John Cassian describes of himself during this early stage of his spirituality:

The Purgative Stage

> In my soul are countless and varied distractions. I am in a fever as my heart moves this way and that. I have no strength to hold in check the scatterings of my thoughts. I cannot utter my prayer without interruption, without being visited by empty images and by the memory of words and doings....[133]

Prayer is often filled with distractions and dryness at this stage because there is a battle going on. There is a battle going on between the anxieties of the world and the peace of Christ. There is a battle going on between self-will and God's will. The *dark nights* will be the purifying fires that will cleanse these aspects of our growth as a spiritual person (these *dark nights* will be discussed more fully in the upcoming chapters). In many ways, in this stage we are divided: We are self-infatuated persons while at the same time struggling Christ-centered persons. The battle between these two aspects of our life is painful and purging. We either do our purgatory in this life or in the next!

Dryness and Distractions

Dryness in prayer is something that needs to be particularly addressed at this stage as well as distractions. I will first deal with the dryness.

One of the most tragic circumstances in the spiritual life is that people of prayer stop praying when dryness enters into their prayer life. Dryness in prayer is associated with the loss of a sense of consolation, peace, happiness, comfort, and good feelings. Where once we were enthusiastic in our prayer life, now we lose this sense and begin to find prayer burdensome. We often remark:

---

[133] *John Cassian: Conferences*, trans. Colm Luibheid (Mahwah: Paulist Press, 1985), Conference 10.

"I'm just too tired to pray tonight. I'll pray another time." In more tragic cases, those who experience dryness for the first time often abandon the spiritual life altogether — this is particularly true of neophytes who are unaware of what is going on in their souls.

Dryness is God's way of purifying our prayer. It is easy to pray when we get "goodies" from God, but God in the dryness of prayer is saying: "I now want you to pray to me out of pure faith. I want you to pray to me for simply being me, not for the 'goodies' you get from me." If we persevere in prayer during this dryness, we will exit the dryness as a person of much more profound spiritual insight. We will experience a newness of life that is associated with progress in the spiritual life and come out of the dryness a better, more powerful, spiritual person. However, the sad reality is that too many fail to persevere through the dryness. They give up too easily.

Hence, many who fail to persevere end up regressing. They stop praying until life becomes very empty. They restart their prayer life and find consolation and all the "goodies" associated with it. But then dryness again sets in, and they again abandon prayer, until they feel a need for it. Life for such people is a continual cycle of progress and regression in the spiritual life. They move a little and then fall back again. They live their lives in this unending cycle which hinders any great sense of fulfillment, peace, contentment, or happiness.

Life is filled with anxieties for such people, for they fail to progress. That is why most Christians live and die in the purgative stage. They fail to persevere in the battle of prayer. They are too willing to fall back on what they perceive as something safer. They fail to trust God enough. They fail to surrender to his will. They fail to realize that God knows what is best for their salvation and happiness. They fail to realize that he is the way, the truth, and the life (cf. Jn 14:6).

Distraction is another factor that hinders most Christians

The Purgative Stage

in the spiritual life. Distractions are brought about by a failure to surrender and trust completely in God.

Consequently, life's problems and anxieties enter into our prayer life. Distractions will slowly diminish as we progress in perseverance in the spiritual life of prayer.

One little technique that can often be used in moments of distractions is to have at hand a favorite word that reminds us of God (e.g., love, peace, hope, and so forth). Whenever the distractions enter into our prayers, then we can call upon this word to help refocus our prayer back on God.

Prayer is a spiritual battle. Let us fight the good fight (cf. 1 Tm 6:12; 2 Tm 4:7).

Beginning to See Christ in Others

While the purgative stage is primarily a self-centered stage, the grace of God is moving us to see in others aspects of Christ, albeit at this stage we only see at a very superficial level. At this stage we are able to see Christ in the great saints, but we have a great deal of trouble seeing Christ in our neighbor. This stage is still a very self-absorbed stage in the spiritual journey.

Backsliding

In the purgative stage of the spiritual journey we are always in danger of backsliding. This is particularly true when we enter the first *dark night*, which will be discussed in the next chapter. Thus, at this stage we must hold onto the gift of faith as our guide.[134] We must hold onto the words of Jesus that remind the

---
[134] Cf. *Ascent*, Bk. II, Ch. 4, nos. 2-3.

world that he came that all "may have life and have it abundantly" (Jn 10:10), and we must hold onto the words of St. Paul that remind us that in Christ all "may be filled with the fullness of God" (Eph 3:19).

The purgative stage of the spiritual journey is a painful one, yet it is not a stage that is without hope or direction. For the faithful one knows that by holding on, by fighting the good fight, by being courageous, by living one day at a time, and by surrendering more and more to God's will, victory and happiness are at hand. Serenity and peace are close by. We must find comfort in a prayer similar to that of Reinhold Niebuhr:

> God grant me the serenity to accept the things I cannot change, courage to change the things I can, and the wisdom to know the difference. Living one day at a time; enjoying one moment at a time; accepting hardships as the pathway to peace. Taking as Jesus did this sinful world as it is, not as I would have it; trusting that He will make all things right if I surrender to His will; that I may be reasonably happy in this life and supremely happy with Him forever in the next.

A person who fails to persevere will find himself or herself permanently trapped in the superficial purgative stage of spirituality, where no lasting authentic peace and contentment can be found, for by its nature this early stage is a painful, purifying stage. Most Christians live and die in this purgative stage. That is why most Christians live and die as superficial Christians.

Failing to move forward is easy for the uncommitted, for it is always easier to go back to where one has been than to go forward into the unknown. The unknown can be frightening, and requires surrendering and trusting in God. Most people are afraid to surrender and to move into the sphere of the unknown, for God may ask them more than they are willing to give!

New vs. Old Self

In Christ we become a new creation (cf. 2 Cor 5:17). The purgative stage is the beginning of this new creative, revolutionary process that is taking place in us.

If we choose to move beyond this point and enter more profoundly into the unknown, into the mystery of God, then we will experience an ever more profound experience of life.

4

The First Dark Night
The Active Purification of the Senses

> The greatest suffering of the souls in purgatory... is their awareness that something in them displeases God, that they have deliberately gone against His great goodness....[135]
> *St. Catherine of Genoa*

Purgatory will have to be done here on earth or in the afterlife, for heaven is a place of perfection. Let us seek to do our purgatory here on earth, for what greater gift of love can we give the Father?

The active purification of the senses is a time of purification that gives liberty to the Spirit. It is a time when a person "pummels [his or her] body and subdues it" (1 Cor 9:27). It is a time when the person's inner being is being prepared for a state of existence where nature and grace complement each other, where the body does not cause any hindrance for the soul. It is a time when a re-directing of one's energies is taking place to fight off occasions of sins. It is a time when sensuality and irritability, which are the hallmarks of this stage of the spiritual journey, are curbed

---

[135] *Catherine of Genoa: Purgation and Purgatory*, trans. Serge Hughs (Mahwah: Paulist Press, 1979), 77f.

by a burning fire.[136] It is a time, as St. Maximus Confessor explains, when a person's "affective drive is wholly directed to God."[137]

This stage is called a *dark night* for it is a time when the senses are deprived of the consolations that are usually associated with a relationship with God. Those who first enter this stage may feel they are falling away from God, but in reality, they are closer to God than ever before in their spiritual journey. God is now asking them to follow him in faith and not out of an infatuation or desire for consolations or "goodies" from God.

The active purification of the senses is a time when we actively seek to purify our being of those things that hinder the spiritual life and ultimately happiness. While grace is clearly present in the process most of the work being done in the purification process is being done by the individual who actively struggles to purify that which is contrary to the glory and honor of God. In this active purification, the imagination, memory, intellect, and will begin to be purified of things that hinder a full experience of God. As William of St. Thierry states:

> Man's part is continually to prepare his heart by ridding his will of foreign attachments, his reason or intellect of anxieties, his memory of idle or absorbing, sometimes even of necessary business, so that in the Lord's good time and when he sees fit, at the sound of the Holy Spirit's breathing, the elements which constitute thought may be free at once to come together and do their work, each contributing its share to the outcome of joy for the soul. The will displays pure affection for the joy which the Lord gives, the memory yields faithful material, the intellect affords the sweetness of experience....[138]

---

[136] Cf. ST IIa IIae, q. 35, a. 1, ad 4um.
[137] *Maximus Confessor: Selected Writings*, trans. George C. Berthold (Mahwah: Paulist Press, 1985), Third Century, n. 98.
[138] *William of St. Thierry: The Golden Epistle*, trans. Theodore Berkeley, O.C.S.O. (Kalamazoo: Cistercian Publications, Inc., 1971), n. 251.

Imagination

A person cannot think without images in this early stage. An image always accompanies an idea. In the active purification of the imagination, the imagination is directed by reason illumined by faith. When the imagination is filled with impurities, the intellect is disrupted and damaged from functioning properly. If the imagination is cleansed from impurities, the imagination complements the intellect in its proper functioning.[139] The imagination is a faculty of great power in the spiritual journey. It is in need of constant purification, even in persons highly advanced in the spiritual life.[140]

Memory[141]

Concupiscence and personal sin cause us to retain dangerous memories, memories that hinder and stunt growth. As St. Maximus Confessor states, "the battle against memories is more difficult than the battle against deeds, as sinning in thought is easier than sinning in deed."[142] An ordered, healthy memory remembers the things of God, and a disordered memory forgets the good that God has done. For example, if we remember the wrongs that another person or persons has done to us, we can at times have trouble forgiving that person or persons. The pain of the memory can preoccupy us with hatred and miserable feelings, and therefore hinder our focus on God.

When we do so we are prone to forget God (cf. Jr 2:32; Ps 105:13, 21). We tend to focus on the here and now as opposed to eternity. We need to heal and order our memory to its proper func-

---

[139] Cf. ST Ia, q. 78, a. 4; q. 84, a. 7.
[140] *Interior Castle*, 5th mansion, Ch. 4; 6th mansion, Ch. 1.
[141] *Ascent*, Bk. III, Chs. 1-15.
[142] *Maximus Confessor: Selected Writings*, First Century, n. 63.

tioning. The theological virtue of hope helps to heal our memory by assisting us to avoid focusing on useless and dangerous recollections. Our mind, directed by hope, turns to God.[143]

Intellect

The intellect can be wounded by concupiscence and personal sin. The wounded intellect leads to ignorance. It is kept from perceiving truth and from grasping higher realities. We become absorbed in earthly considerations. When our intellect is wounded we are apt to neglect the things of God and salvation. We are prone to intellectual and spiritual pride and sloth, indifference, rash judgments, and spiritual and intellectual blindness. When our intellect is wounded we are not willing to consult others, and are not willing to listen to opposing opinions. We think we know it all (Mt 23:16, 23f).[144]

The infused virtue of faith is the cure for a wounded intellect.[145] Faith is superior to reason and the senses. It enlightens reason, makes us adhere to truths and helps us judge according to these truths. Faith seeks understanding and the understanding that flows from this faith in turn nourishes the fruitfulness of faith.[146]

Will

The will is the faculty that tends toward the good known through the intellect. It has for its object the universal good that permits it to rise to the love of God. The will makes use of the

---

[143] *Ascent*, Bk. II, Chs. 10, 11, 16, 22; Bk. III, Chs. 6f. and 14.
[144] ST Ia IIae, q. 85, a. 3; IIa IIae, q. 15; q. 35, a. 4, ad 3um; q. 138; q. 167, a. 1.
[145] ST IIa IIae, q. 7, a. 2; *Ascent*, Bk. III, 6f.
[146] *Ascent*, Bk. II, Chs. 3, 9, 11.

The First Dark Night

other faculties, especially the intellect and the imagination, in guiding us to the good.[147]

Concupiscence and personal sin cause defects in the will. Self-centeredness and egoism are the greatest wounds to the will. They lead us to forget the love of God and neighbor. They lead to thoughtlessness, agitation, discouragement, dissension, trouble, and anxiety. They lead to a battle wherein we try to control God. They make us flee from all that requires sacrifice.

The cure for these wounds is found in the infused virtue of love.[148] Love moves us from being self-centered and ego-centered to other-centered. We become, through authentic love, a person for others.

> Take, Lord, and receive all my liberty, my memory, my understanding, and my entire will, all that I have and possess. You have given all to me; to you, O Lord, now I return it; all is yours. Dispose of me wholly according to your Will. Give me only your love and your grace, for this is enough for me. *St. Ignatius of Loyola*

---

[147] Cf. ST Ia, q. 80, a. 1f.
[148] *Ascent*, Bk. II, 6f.

5

The Second Part of the First Dark Night
The Passive Purification of the Senses

> Lead, Kindly Light, amid the encircling gloom
> Lead Thou me on!
> The Night is dark, and I am far from home —
> Lead Thou me on!
> Keep Thou my feet; I do not ask to see
> The distant scene — one step enough for me.
> I was not ever thus, nor pray'd that Thou
> Shouldst lead me on.
> I loved to choose and see my path, but now
> Lead Thou me on.
> I loved the garish day, and, spite of fears,
> Pride ruled my will: remember not past years.
> So long Thy power hath blest me, sure it still
> Will lead me on,
> O'er moor and fen, o'er crag and torrent, till
> The night is gone;
> And with the morn those angel faces smile
> Which I have loved long since, and lost awhile.[149]
>
> *John Henry Newman*

---

[149] John Henry Newman, *Verses on Various Occasions* (London: Longmans, Green, and Co., 1910), 156-157.

In the active purification of the senses, we did most of the work in response to grace in purifying the senses of all that was not for the honor and glory of God. Now in the passive purification, God is doing most of the work.[150]

In the passive purification of the senses, we move from an imperfect stage in our relationship with God, one where self-interest and self-satisfaction are the main emphasis, to a more perfect stage, where our main emphasis is starting to be God-centered. Our emphasis is on, "What can I do for God?" as opposed to "What can God do for me?"[151]

The signs of this stage are well described by St. John of the Cross:[152]

1) We find no comfort in the things of God or in the things of the world. Our focus is no longer on the desires of the senses for their own sake. It is a time when we must will our being through this period of dryness.

2) Anxiety is symptomatic of this period of purification. We feel a sense that we are not serving God. In fact, we even sense that we are going backwards in the spiritual journey. We can become sluggish, weak, and even depressed in our journey. Yet the desire, the will, continues to move us forward in serving God.

3) An inability to meditate, to reflect, and to excite the imagination are the hallmarks of this stage. God is beginning to be primarily experienced by means of the spirit as opposed to that of the senses.

It is crucially important to recognize that *all three* conditions must exist in the person at the *same time*; otherwise, what we are

---

[150] *Dark Night*, Bk. I, Ch. 3.
[151] Cf. St. Catherine of Siena, *Dialogue*, Chs. 75, 144, 149.
[152] *Dark Night*, Bk. I, Ch. 9; *Ascent*, Bk. II, Chs. 13f.

The Second Part of the First Dark Night

dealing with most likely is the result of a sinful life or a life wounded by a medical or psychological problem.

Initial Infused Contemplation

> When the mind receives the representations of things, it of course patterns itself after each representation. In contemplating them spiritually it is variously conformed to each object contemplated. But when it comes to be in God, it becomes wholly without form and pattern, for in contemplating the one who is simple it becomes simple and entirely patterned in light.[153]   *St. Maximus Confessor*

God at this stage is transforming meditation into a higher form of prayer, initial infused contemplation. Contemplation transfers to the core of the person in a more profound manner the goods and energies which once were solely attained through the senses. Furthermore, it transfers to the core of the person spiritual gifts and strengths that transcend the ability of the internal and external senses to experience, because by its very nature contemplation is beyond the limits of the imagination and the gift of natural reason. It is because the gift of contemplation transcends the limits of the imagination and the gift of reason that the senses experience a sense of dryness, a sense of void. The reality is, however, that God is closest to the person at this stage for he is asking the person to love him in pure faith as opposed to loving him for the good things he gives.

In this initial stage of contemplation, we are not yet completely aware of what is going on. All that we are aware of is that there is an inner desire for solitude and quiet.

---

[153] *Maximus Confessor: Selected Writings*, Third Century, n. 97.

While we have begun to enter into the initial sphere of contemplation at this stage of the spiritual life, we have not completely become removed from the ability to enter into discursive meditation. In fact, at this stage, it is not unusual for us to move back and forth between meditation and contemplation. When meditation is fruitful, then we should remain at this stage of prayer until God moves us forward. If meditation becomes dry, then we are being moved in grace to contemplation.[154]

Contemplation is fruitful when it becomes less and less distracted by concepts or thoughts. When we become overly burdened by these distractions, God is calling us back to the state of meditation. When we feel an inability to meditate, to use concepts and thoughts in prayer, then we are being called to contemplation.[155]

The Jesus Prayer

The *Jesus Prayer* is often helpful during this transition from meditation to initial infused contemplation. The *Jesus Prayer* is the unceasing repetition of the phrase "Lord Jesus Christ, Son of God, have mercy on me a sinner." We seek during this repetition to find a state where we gaze upon the heart of God without images or idle thoughts.[156]

Centering Prayer/Technique

Centering prayer is a powerful gift at this stage of the spiritual life. St. Teresa of Avila alludes to this reality in chapter 31,7

---

[154] Cf. *Dark Night*, Bk. I, Ch. 10; *Ascent*, Bk. II, Ch. 13; *Life*, Ch. 14.
[155] Cf. Evagrius Ponticus, *The 153 Chapters on Prayer*, 9, 44, 69-70, 120.
[156] See *John Climacus: The Ladder of Divine Ascent*, trans. Colm Luibheid (Mahwah: Paulist Press, 1982), 103, 239, 262, 266, 274-276, 278-279, 286, 290.

of her book *The Way of Perfection*. Centering prayer is a technique whereby a person chooses a favorite word, "a gentle word" (or even an image) that reminds him or her of God and then uses this word or image to chase away distractions to contemplative prayer. At this initial stage of infused contemplation, distractions are normal; hence, a centering word or image can help, in grace, to move us into a deeper experience of contemplation.

Gifts of the Spirit

The gifts of the Spirit are flowering at this point, particularly the gifts of knowledge, understanding, fortitude, and the fear of the Lord.

Knowledge

We begin to know that the things of the world are empty unless they are directed to the glory and honor of God.[157]

Understanding

We begin to penetrate the deeper aspects of the faith. We are cleansing our experience of the faith of all phantasms, misrepresentations, and errors. We are moving beyond simple adherence to formulas and the simple recitation of prayers, to a more penetrating experience of those formulas and recited prayers.[158]

Fortitude

The desire to serve God at all cost is beginning to take effect. We find ourselves willing to follow in Christ's footsteps and

---

[157] ST IIa IIae, q. 9, a. 4.
[158] ST IIa IIae, q. 8, a. 7; q. 61, a. 5.

carry the cross. The virtues of patience and longanimity are enhanced by this gift as we manage the trials and tribulations of life with Christ-like courage.[159]

Fear of the Lord

This gift of the Spirit makes us fear sin. "My flesh trembles for fear of thee, and I am afraid of thy judgments" (Ps 118:120). This gift profoundly strengthens us to live a virtuous, patient and chaste life out of fear of being condemned to hell.[160] Sins against chastity and patience are the hallmark of this level of the spiritual life.[161] When we enter into the deeper stages of the spiritual life, the fear of hell will be replaced by the fear of not loving enough.

How to Get Out of the Dark Night

St. John of the Cross teaches his disciples how to progress through the *dark night*:[162]

1) They must have an enlightened spiritual director.
2) They must persevere in patience, trust, and humility through this difficult time.
3) They must keep focused on Jesus and his cross.
4) They must foster a docile spirit and be open to God's providence.
5) They must will themselves through this period of purification in faith.

---

[159] Cf. ST IIa IIae, q. 139, a. 2.
[160] Cf. ST IIa IIae, q. 19, a. 9, a. 19.
[161] *Dark Night*, Bk. I, Ch. 14.
[162] *Dark Night*, Ch. 10.

The Second Part of the First Dark Night

The Effects of the Passive Purification of the Senses

The passive purification of the senses has subjected the senses to the Spirit. Our senses have been spiritualized. We are moved more by an attraction to God for being God as opposed to God for being a giver of things. We begin to have a profound knowledge of God and self. We become aware of a new sense of power in fighting sin and in penetrating the mysteries of God. We begin to see the world and our being as never before. We are entering the sphere of enlightenment.[163] We are entering the sphere of dependence on God and a joyful surrendering to God's will.

The Dark Night and Psychological Considerations

The *dark night* of the senses and the *dark night* of the soul (which will be discussed just before the unitive stage) can be very confusing to people who are experiencing them and who are observing them. This is a very delicate and crucial time in the spiritual journey. Great harm can be done by spiritual directors, psychologists, and psychiatrists if they are not aware of what is going on. The sad reality of today is that most priests are inadequately trained in the field of spirituality and in the field of psychology or psychiatry, and the same can be said of psychologists and psychiatrists: most lack an understanding of spiritual theology. Hence, great harm can be caused to the person's spiritual journey, either by retarding their progress or leaving them in a stupor of uncertainty and confusion, when improper advice is given. It is of great relief that the Roman schools of theology have greatly emphasized this interaction between the psychological and the spiritual. It is my hope that this will filter down to all seminaries in the training of priests.

---

[163] Cf. *Dark Night*, Chs. 12 and 13; Catherine of Siena, *Dialogue*, Ch. 4; *Life*, Ch. 31.

Given what has been said, it is unrealistic to expect a priest to have adequate training in the field of psychology or psychiatry, given that the most basic training of priests takes nine to ten years. Likewise, it is unrealistic for psychologists and psychiatrists to have an adequate training in spiritual theology, given their own extensive years of studies. The solution is to seek out a cooperative interaction in the counseling of persons. As the cliché goes: Two minds are better than one. A person can rightly claim, therefore, that two or three fields of study are better than one.

What is the harm that can be done by the misdiagnosis of a person? The danger for the uninformed spiritual director is that what may very well be a pathological condition in need of either psychological counseling or psychiatric help in the form of medication, or both, can be left untreated. The person in such a case may in fact not be experiencing a *dark night* at all. They may rather be experiencing a psychological breakdown or the results of a chemical imbalance. Failure to bring this to the attention of a psychologist or psychiatrist can be extremely harmful to the person. On the other hand, if a person is experiencing an authentic *dark night* then the use of medication can be extremely detrimental to the progress of the person, for the medication could very well eliminate the very function of the *dark night*, the purification of the person's being.

Purification is by its very nature a painful experience. To medicate the painful experience so that the individual experiences only bliss will retard the very purpose of the *dark night*. It will definitely stifle the purgative process and can in fact lead the person to regress to a lower stage in the spiritual life.

A final point to be made is that at times, a person authentically experiencing a *dark night* may also be experiencing a pathological disorder. This is a case where the close interaction of the spiritual director and the psychologist or psychiatrist is essential. Having said all this, the following is a brief guideline in helping

The Second Part of the First Dark Night

to understand what is authentically a part of the *dark night* and what is more of a psychological or pathological problem.

Faith, hope, and love are the distinguishing marks between the *dark nights* and patently pathological conditions.

In the *dark nights*, no matter how bad things get, even to the edge of despair, there is always a sense of faith and hope, a sense that one will be able to will one's self through the situation in grace. There is a sense of trust that God is in control and that even though a person may not be clear as to where God is taking him or her, there is the clear understanding that God will not abandon the person. The will and trust — empowered by grace — to move on is never extinguished no matter how bad things get. Furthermore, and more importantly, the person never loses a sense of the love of God or of neighbor in the *dark nights*. No matter how wrenching the pain of the purgation, the love of God remains and the love of neighbor remains. The striving for being a person for others always remains. Humility, patience, and calm grow during these *dark nights* — particularly when the individual is in the hands of a competent spiritual director.

In a pathological situation, the faith of a person is deeply damaged and can be lost at an explicit level. The ability to will one's being through the situation is often impossible. Trust is often lost. The future looks bleak. There is seemingly no hope, without a drastic change. Love of neighbor is often replaced by a dislike or hate for others. The individual becomes excessively or obsessively introspective or self-absorbed to the point of losing sight of concerns for others. They can become implicitly and even explicitly the center of the universe in their outlook. Love of God is often turned into a sense of indifference or even bitter anger toward him. The sense of being purged is often replaced with the sense of being cursed. The person can begin to lose a grip on reality.

These key factors, when explored by competent individuals

in the fields of spirituality, psychology, and psychiatry, are of great importance in determining whether one is experiencing a *dark night* or whether one is experiencing a pathological disturbance.

The ultimate sign that a person has gone through the *dark night* is that he or she comes out of it renewed and prepared for a deeper prayer and spiritual life. The ultimate sign that one has not gone through a *dark night* is that he or she becomes increasingly ill, with no cure in sight, until they turn to professional help.

The Illuminative Stage
A Time of Enlightenment

Again Jesus spoke to them, saying, "I am the light of the world; he who follows me will not walk in darkness, but will have the light of life" (Jn 8:12).

In the purgative stage we grow to love God with our whole heart primarily by means of the faculties of the senses. In the illuminative stage we begin to love God not only with our whole heart, but also with our whole soul. This love transcends the limits of the senses. In the final stage, the unitive stage of the spiritual journey, love becomes complete. At this stage we love God with our whole heart, soul, strength, and mind.

In the illuminative stage, the ease of prayer returns after the darkness. A greater capacity for work, service, teaching, directing, and organizing takes place at this stage. The illuminative stage is exemplified by "good works." It is the beginning of the mystical life. It is the time when everyday mysticism is experienced. As Karl Rahner states, it is a stage in life

- where we dare to pray into silent darkness and know that we are heard, although no answer seems to come back about which we might argue and rationalize,

- where we let ourselves go unconditionally and experience this capitulation as true victory,
- where falling becomes true uprightness,
- where desperation is accepted and is still secretly accepted as trustworthy without cheap trust,
- where we entrust all our knowledge and all our questions to the silent and all-inclusive mystery which is loved more than all our individual knowledge which makes us such small people,
- where we rehearse our death in everyday life and try to live in such a way as we would like to die, peaceful and composed....[164]

This is the mystical walk with and in God. This is the "mysticism of everyday life."

In the illuminative stage, the acquired virtues that were primarily predominant in the purgative stage are now brought to the service of the infused virtues. The acquired virtues and the infused virtues, therefore, work hand in hand for the good of the person's growth in the life of God.[165]

The virtues come together as never before in the illuminative stage. The acquired virtue of prudence and the infused virtue of prudence work hand in hand and are aided by the Spirit's gift of counsel. The fruits of this interaction are foresight, circumspection, and constancy. The acquired virtue of fortitude and the infused virtue of fortitude work hand in hand and are aided by the Spirit's gift of fortitude. The fruits of this interaction are patience, magnanimity, and longanimity. The acquired virtue of justice and the infused virtue of justice work hand in hand and are aided by

---

[164] Karl Rahner, *The Spirit in the Church*, trans. John Griffiths (New York: The Seabury Press, 1979), 21-22.
[165] Cf. ST Ia IIae, q. 63, a. 4.

the Spirit's gift of piety. The fruits of this interaction are obedience and a call for penance and religion. The acquired virtue of temperance and the infused virtue of temperance work hand in hand and are aided by the Spirit's gift of fear. The fruits of this interaction are chastity, meekness, and poverty.[166]

Acquired Prudence (cf. Pr 14:15; 1 P 4:7)

> The mind that has succeeded in the active life advances in prudence....[167]
> *St. Maximus Confessor*

Acquired prudence is the moral virtue that directs through right reason acts of justice, courage, temperance, and their related virtues. It preserves us from impulsiveness in temperament, imagination, and sensible appetites. It moves us to seek advice, obey what is reasonable, and gives the strength to deal with differences in the temperament of different characters. At this stage of the spiritual journey, the acquired virtue of prudence is well developed and prepares us for the powerful response to the infused gift of prudence, the moral virtue that is grace-elevated.[168]

Infused Prudence

Infused prudence is the moral virtue that transcends the limits of the natural gift of right reason. It is in a sense the consequence of taking an acquired moral virtue and infusing it with grace. Grace elevates that which was natural into the realm of that which is supernatural. The infused moral virtue of prudence is given in response to grace. It is marked by a profound love and

---

[166] Cf. ST Ia IIae, q. 63, a. 4.
[167] *Maximus Confessor: Selected Writings*, Second Century, n. 26.
[168] Cf. ST Ia IIae, q. 58, a. 5; q. 64, a. 1.

zeal for God and for the burning desire for the salvation and good of all people. It directs all the virtues to that which can be considered their last end, which is God's eternal destiny for all. All acts are judged according to a pilgrim's eternal destiny. The focus is on eternity, and not simply on the temporal aspects of life, which the acquired virtues tend to be primarily focused on.[169]

The gift of counsel accompanies the infused moral virtue of prudence. Wise decisions are made which are based on the knowledge of self and God. This leads to mercy, the beatitude of mercy, for a person with the infused moral virtue of prudence is able to strike a comfortable balance between rigor and justice. It also leads to the preferential option for mercy.[170]

Foresight, circumspection, and constancy are the quintessential marks of a person with prudence in the illuminative stage of the spiritual journey. They are blessed with an elevated sense of foresight and circumspection; that is, that grace-empowered ability to consider all circumstances and their possible consequences, particularly as they pertain to one's eternal destiny. They are also blessed with the gift of constancy, that ability to remain — as a consequence of the insights brought about through foresight and circumspection — steadfast in faith in whatever life may bring.[171]

Prudence and Simplicity

Prudence moves us to live life simply. Prudence enables us to do the littlest things in the holiest manner.[172] St. Thérèse of Lisieux's *little way* exemplifies this reality.

---

[169] Cf. ST Ia, q. 79, a. 9.
[170] Cf. ST IIa IIae, q. 52, a. 4.
[171] Cf. ST Ia IIae, q. 63, a. 4.
[172] Cf. ST IIa IIae, q. 109, a. 2 ad 4um.

The Illuminative Stage

Acquired and Infused Fortitude

The acquired moral virtue of courage or fortitude is elevated by grace into the realm of infused courage or fortitude. Aided by the Spirit's gift of fortitude, the moral virtue of fortitude raises us to new heights in the spiritual life, to new heights in patience, magnanimity, and longanimity or forbearance. Those experiencing the grace of fortitude are those whose patience in times of difficulty does not allow them to depart from right reason illumined by faith. They have the patience and forbearance to endure and fight off any temptations that might cause them to yield to difficulties. At this stage we are able to bear, often beyond the natural abilities of the body, adversity, sadness, and injuries of all sorts for whatever length of time.

We are able to see and bear the cross. This seeing and bearing of the cross is done with magnanimity, with a sense of calm and sacrifice. The end of the difficulty is seen, the victory of the cross is clearly perceived by us. Because of this reality, we experience a loftiness of spirit enabling us to disdain any hint of meanness or revenge as a consequence of the adversity encountered.[173]

Acquired and Infused Justice

Justice is a movement away from self-infatuation and a movement toward the good of others (cf. Lv 19:15; Col 4:1). Again, as with all the moral virtues, the acquired moral virtue of justice is at the service of the infused, grace-filled, moral virtue of justice. Aided by the Spirit's gift of piety, we exemplify a life of authentic faith and works.[174]

When discussing the moral virtue of justice, we must take

---

[173] Cf. ST IIa IIae, q. 136, a. 1.
[174] Cf. ST Ia IIae, q. 56, a. 6, c and ad 3um.

into account the three expressions of justice that a person at this stage of the spiritual journey is radically aware of.

1) *Commutative Justice*: Commutative justice is aimed at the dignity of equality. Because of this reality, it is a form of justice that fights against any occurrences of theft, fraud, usury, false accusations, insults, unjust blame, defamation, slander, gossip, insinuation, and so on.[175]
2) *Distributive Justice*: Distributive justice is aimed at how public goods are used. It fights against any hint of favoritism, oppression, unrelieved poverty, and corruption of all kinds.[176]
3) *Social Justice*: Social justice or legal justice is preoccupied with the common good of society. It demands personal sacrifice,[177] and is inseparable from prayer:

> Action and contemplation now grow together into one life and one unity. They become two aspects of the same thing. Action is charity looking outward to other men, and contemplation is charity drawn inward to its own divine source. Action is the stream, and contemplation is the spring. The spring remains more important than the stream, for the only thing that really matters is for love to spring up inexhaustibly from the infinite abyss of Christ and of God.[178] *Thomas Merton*

Guiding all three of these expressions of justice is the gift of *epikeia*, the gift that preserves the dignity of the human person at all cost, the gift that recognizes the spirit as well as the letter of the law.[179]

---

[175] Cf. ST IIa IIae, q. 73-75.
[176] Cf. ST IIa IIae, q. 63, a. 1f.
[177] Cf. ST IIa IIae, q. 58, a. 6f.
[178] Merton, *No Man Is an Island* (New York: Image Books, 1967), 65.
[179] Cf. ST IIa IIae, q. 120, a. 1f.

Justice and Veracity

Justice and veracity are intertwined with prudence and simplicity. Justice and veracity however are predominantly concerned with moral integrity, with telling the truth and acting according to it. In the illuminative stage sins of duplicity, hypocrisy, boasting, and mockery are extinguished.[180] There are no two-faced saints!

Acquired and Infused Temperance

Temperance elevated by grace to what is referred to as infused temperance — and aided by the Spirit's gift of fear — is the moral virtue that is exemplified by a sense of moderation in thought, action and feeling (cf. Si 5:2; 18:30; 37:27-31; Tt 2:12). Temperance finds its most precious expression in the evangelical counsels[181] of poverty, chastity, and obedience. Meekness (that ability to endure persecutions or injustices with patience and without resentment) is also a significant expression at this stage of the spiritual journey.

The Evangelical Counsels

Poverty is the gift that purifies us of all attachments. It is the gift that unites us to Christ Jesus. For St. Thomas Aquinas, Christ chose a life of poverty for four reasons, four reasons that all disciples are all called to imitate.[182]

---

[180] Cf. ST IIa IIae, q. 109, a. 2 ad 4um.
[181] The evangelical counsels are responsible for the majority of the grace-filled work of detachment that is necessary for holiness and thus happiness.
[182] ST IIIa, q. 40, a. 3; q. 35, a. 7.

1) Poverty frees us from the cares that are associated with earthly goods.
2) Poverty frees us to be concerned with the salvation of souls.
3) Poverty frees us for the desire of eternal goods.
4) Poverty frees us, in the absence and contradiction of earthly helps, to express the divine power that saves souls.

Poverty is true freedom. It moves the clouds of worldly attachments away from the spiritual life and detaches us from all that is not for the glory and honor of God. Love of God, love of neighbor and love of heaven are the all-consuming hungers of the poor in spirit.[183]

Chastity of heart and body are exemplified in the infused moral virtue of temperance. Whether one is a virgin, a religious, or a single, unmarried person, all are called to a chaste life, a life free of lewdness or salaciousness, a life which is pure in thought and action. It is empowered by the grace that accompanies the love of neighbor and the love of God.[184]

Obedience is a joyful submissiveness to that which is best for our eternal salvation. Obedience delivers us from the slavery that is attached to self-will and self-infatuation. The fruits of obedience, thus, are rectitude, or righteousness in judgment, which is accompanied by a liberty of spirit: "Now the Lord is the Spirit, and where the Spirit of the Lord is, there is freedom" (2 Cor 3:17).

Theological Virtues of Faith, Hope and Love

Faith

Faith is a gift (Eph 2:8) aided by the gift of understanding which is in conformity with reason, yet transcends the limits of

---
[183] Cf. ST IIa, q. 23, a. 1, ad 3um.
[184] Cf. ST IIa IIae, q. 151, a. 1-3.

reason.[185] Faith in the illuminative stage is freed to a great extent of all aspects of egoism, passions, jealousies, whims, etc., of all that can damage our response to the inner call of grace. For some at this stage, faith is greater in the faculty of the intellect, thereby producing the fruits of certitude and firmness in actions. In others, faith is greater in the will, thereby producing the fruits of devotion and confidence.[186] In either case, all aspects of life are being guided by the light of faith, which guides the individual to his or her eternal destiny of loving God for being God (Rm 8:28).

Hope

Hope is confidence in the help of God. Hope helps us to persevere (Mt 10:22) and overcome trials and tribulations (Rm 5:2-5). Hope, because of these trials and tribulations, purifies us for the love of God (cf. Ws 3:4-6). Hope is a walk into the mystery of the unknown. Yet it is a walk with a certain sense of certitude of direction. Hope makes us advance always more generously toward God by giving us a greater desire for him. God becomes our end; God becomes all that is hoped for.

In the illuminative stage two lingering defects from the purgative stage are being polished off: *presumption and discouragement.* Presumption is the defect that fails to recognize the necessity of responding to grace in the spiritual journey. It is the defect that overemphasizes God's mercy, and underemphasizes God's justice. Hence, people often feel they can be pardoned without repentance or in the worst case they can even feel assured of salvation no matter what they do. In the case of the defect of discouragement at this stage, we can often feel that the spiritual journey is too difficult and thus hopeless. We may turn away from grace and go back to

---

[185] Cf. ST IIa IIae, q. 15.
[186] ST IIa IIae, q. 5, a. 4.

our former way of life because we sense that grace is too inaccessible. In the illuminative stage these two hideous defects against hope, against properly ordered confidence in God, are being completely finished off, completely extinguished.

Love

For John Climacus, "Love, by its nature, is a resemblance to God."[187] Love is the conformity of our will to God's, for all the other virtues follow the virtue of love (cf. 1 Cor 13:4). In the illuminative stage, certain signs can be seen according to St. Thomas Aquinas:[188]

1) Mortal sins are a thing of the past, since love has conquered that inclination.
2) Because of love, earthly things such as pleasures, honors, wealth, etc., are no longer of great interest.
3) Because of love, we seek to be engulfed in the presence of God, to love him, to think of him, to adore him, to pray to him, to thank him, to ask his pardon, to aspire to him.
4) We desire, out of the grace of love, to please God more than anything and anyone in the entire created realm of reality.
5) We seek to love and know God in our neighbor, in spite of the neighbor's defects. We love our neighbor for simply being a child of God, a child of God who is beloved by God. In the illuminative stage we love God in our neighbor and our neighbor in God. Love of God and love of neighbor merge into one reality.

In the words of Dorothy Day, "We cannot love God unless we love each other, and to love we must know each other."[189] Love

---

[187] *John Climacus: The Ladder of Divine Ascent*, Step. 30, 286.
[188] ST Ia IIae, q. 112, a. 5.
[189] Day, *The Long Loneliness*, 317.

of neighbor is the most distinguishing characteristic of the illuminative stage (cf. Mt 5:44, 47, 48).

Zeal

> Dearest Lord, teach me to be generous. Teach me to serve You as You deserve; to give and not to count the cost; to fight and not to heed the wounds; to toil and not to seek for rest; to labor and not to ask for reward, save that of knowing that I am doing Your will. Amen.
> *St. Ignatius of Loyola*

The illuminative stage of the spiritual journey is marked with tremendous zeal. It is a holy zeal that is directed toward the glory and honor of God and in particular the salvation of all people. Unlike the zeal that is predominant in the purgative stage, this zeal is not lost during times of trials and tribulations, nor is it susceptible to bitterness.

Motives for Zeal

Zeal is nourished by a deep grace-filled thirst to love God and neighbor above all. It is signified by the following marks:

1) An intense desire to imitate Christ in all things.
2) An intense desire to bring all people into the kingdom of God.
3) An intense desire to overcome the enemies of the Church.
4) An intense desire to overcome indifference, inertia, lack of comprehension, ill will, and spiteful opposition.

Qualities of Holy Zeal

Holy zeal is enlightened by the light of faith. It is the fruit of the acquired and infused moral virtues, particularly the virtue of prudence and the gifts of the Holy Spirit, particularly the gifts of wisdom and counsel. Unlike bitter zeal, which is not of God, and which is self-seeking, proud, insensitive, impatient, rude and hate-filled, holy zeal, which is of God, is calm, humble, meek, patient, sensitive, and always other-centered. This type of zeal is expressed in the traditional spiritual and corporal works of mercy:

Corporal Works of Mercy

- Feeding the hungry
- Giving drink to the thirsty
- Clothing the naked
- Sheltering the homeless
- Visiting the sick
- Visiting the imprisoned

Spiritual Works of Mercy

- Instructing the ignorant
- Correcting sinners
- Advising the doubtful
- Showing patience to sinners and those in error
- Forgiving others
- Confronting the afflicted
- Praying for the living and the dead

In her fight against the injustices of the world, Dorothy Day could say with great ease: "It is natural for me to stand my ground... using... weapons as the works of mercy to show love and alleviate suffering."[190]

---

[190] Day, *The Long Loneliness*, 206.

The Illuminative Stage

The Holy Spirit in the Illuminative Stage

Wisdom, the highest of the gifts of the Spirit, at this stage of the spiritual life is very active in directing all the other gifts in the grace-filled, zeal-driven, saint of God.[191]

Fear

The gift of fear supplies strength for the imperfections found in the virtues of temperance and chastity. In the purgative stage, the gift of fear tends to be one that is more servile in nature; that is, a person grows in the spiritual life out of a fear of eternal damnation. In the illuminative stage, the gift of fear is transformed into what has been traditionally called filial fear; that is, a fear that empowers the spiritual life not so much out of a fear of hell as much as a fear of not loving enough. For the people at this stage, the big fear consists in having to face Jesus after their earthly journey without having loved enough.

Love for the poor becomes very powerful at this stage, and thus the gift of fear in the illuminative stage is tied to the beatitude of the love for the poor.[192] St. Vincent de Paul would say: "it is better to feed the poor than to raise the dead."

Piety

The gift of piety is the gift of rendering to God what is rightly due to God. Human reason becomes illumined by faith at this stage as never before. Suffering takes on meaning and a sense of sweetness.[193] As John Henry Newman explains, "I am, I can never

---

[191] ST Ia IIae, q. 68, a. 7.
[192] ST Ia IIae, q. 19.
[193] Cf. ST IIa IIae, q. 121.

be thrown away. If I am in sickness, my sickness may serve Him; in perplexity, my perplexity may serve Him; if I am in sorrow, my sorrow may serve Him."[194] At this stage we find in the mystery of suffering the mystery of love, and we find in the mystery of love the mystery of suffering.

Prayer becomes more fervent and persistent as new insights into the mystery of life become illumined. Any hint of hardness of heart is replaced with an open heart. This predisposes us to being open to interior silence, recollection, and detachment. The gift of piety corresponds, as a consequence, to the beatitude that emphasizes the power and preciousness of the meek.[195]

Knowledge

The gift of knowledge is a gift that elevates human knowledge to new heights. At this stage there is a radical knowledge of those things that are of God and those things that are not of God. The knowledge of good and evil is powerfully perceived and felt at this stage. In the illuminative stage, the gift of knowledge is powerfully tied to the beatitude of the sorrowful.[196]

Fortitude

In the illuminative stage there is a heightened desire to fight the temptations of the flesh, the world, and the devil. There is also a heightened degree of patience and perseverance in the quest for justice. This stage is often associated with the beatitude regarding those who hunger and thirst for justice.[197]

---

[194] John Henry Newman, *Meditations and Devotions* (Westminster, MD: Christian Classics, 1975), 301.
[195] Cf. ST IIa IIae, q. 121.
[196] Cf. ST IIa IIae, q. 9.
[197] Cf. ST IIa IIae, q. 139, a. 1, 2.

Counsel

This gift supplies for the imperfections that hinder the virtue of prudence. It corresponds to the beatitude of the merciful, in that all actions are decided in favor of authentic mercy, a mercy that is properly balanced with justice. The gift of counsel at this stage also helps avoid the dangers of temerity, of recklessness and rashness, which often lead to unhealthy and even evil fanaticism. On the other hand, the gift of counsel helps to fight the danger of pusillanimity — that is, cowardliness and timidity in the face of danger or opposition.[198]

Understanding

Understanding in the illuminative stage is enlightened by the interior light of grace. Its primary impact in this stage of a person's journey is in helping to eliminate the imperfections that hinder the deep penetrations into the truths of faith. The gift of understanding is primarily directed to the purification of one's intentions; thus, it is often viewed to correspond to the beatitude of the pure of heart.[199] This purity of heart and deep penetration into the faith can be seen in St. Hildegard of Bingen's reflection on the nature of the Trinity:

> [As] the flame of a fire has three qualities, so there is one God in three Persons. How? A flame is made up of a brilliant light and red power and fiery heat. It has brilliant light that it may shine, and red power that it may endure, and fiery heat that it may burn. Therefore, by the brilliant light understand the Father, Who with paternal love opens His brightness to His faithful; and by the red power, which is

---
[198] Cf. ST IIa IIae, q. 139, a. 1, 2.
[199] Cf. ST IIa IIae, q. 8, a. 1, 4, 6, 7.

in the flame that it may be strong, understand the Son, Who took on a body born from a Virgin, in which His divine wonders are shown; and by the fiery heat understand the Holy Spirit, Who burns ardently in the minds of the faithful. But there is no flame seen where there is neither brilliant light nor red power nor fiery heat; and thus also where neither the Father nor the Son nor the Holy Spirit is known God is not properly worshipped.[200]

Wisdom

> Eternal Wisdom shall be my bride, and I will be her Servitor. Oh God, if I could catch one glimpse of her, speak to her for a few moments.[201]   *Henry Suso*

The highest of the gifts of the Spirit, wisdom, helps us judge all things in relation to God. Since all is seen in terms of God's providence and his will, then, in this stage of the spiritual journey, we experience a sense of peace.[202] In the words of Dorothy Day,

> I should know by this time that just because I feel that everything is useless and going to pieces and badly done and futile, it is not really that way at all. Everything is all right. It is in the hands of God. Let us abandon everything to Divine Providence.[203]

Wisdom brings about peace. We are in peace and we seek to bring this peace to others. This gift corresponds, therefore, to the beatitude of the peacemakers.[204]

---

[200] *Hildegard of Bingen: Scivias*, trans. Mother Columba Hart and Jane Bishop (Mahwah: Paulist Press, 1990), Bk. II, Vision II, n. 6.
[201] *Henry Suso's Life*, in *Exemplar: Life and Writings of Blessed Henry Suso* (Dubuque: Priory Press, 1962), vol. I, 3.
[202] Cf. ST IIa IIae, q. 45, a. 1, 2, 5, 6.
[203] Dorothy Day, *House of Hospitality* (New York: Sheed and Ward, 1939), 101.
[204] Cf. ST IIa IIae, q. 45, a. 1, 2, 5, 6.

The Illuminative Stage

The Ten Commandments (Ex 20:2-17; Dt 5:26)

Through the working of the commandments the mind puts off the passions.[205]   *St. Maximus Confessor*

The first commandment calls one to love God and only God as God.[206] In the purgative stage of spirituality the focus was on properly praying to God with a sense of adoration, obedience, and faithfulness at a superficial level. In the illuminative stage the implications of this adoration, obedience, and faithfulness take on new dimensions. Acts of superstition, divination, and magic that were once thought of as simply acts of innocence or ignorance, are now seen for what they truly are: they are seen as abominable acts which divert spiritual energy from where it authentically belongs, in God. Acts of idolatry such as the subconscious worship of money, power, fame, and worldly accomplishments are seen as empty and unfulfilling. In many ways, money, power, fame, worldly accomplishments, and so forth, become a terrible burden to bear. Atheism and agnosticism, another grave violation of the first commandment, become seen as the worship of self as opposed to that which transcends the self. In the illuminative stage, the fuller dimensions of the first commandment become enlightened.

The second commandment demands a respect for the sacredness of the Lord's name.[207] In the purgative stage, this is often violated by acts of blasphemy, the taking of false oaths, and in acts of perjury. In the illuminative stage, and all subsequent stages, the emphasis is on recognizing all the things of God, including his name, as sacred (cf. Ph 2:10).

The third commandment is a summons to keep the Lord's

---

[205] *Maximus Confessor: Selected Writings*, First Century, n. 94.
[206] Cf. CCC 2084-2132.
[207] Cf. CCC 2142-2155.

Day a holy day.[208] In the purgative stage this often meant the keeping of the Sunday obligation. People at this stage are often late to Mass and often the first out to the parking lot. What is experienced in the Church is very superficially experienced. The emphasis is on keeping an obligation, avoiding hell, and continuing on with a more or less superficial Christian experience of life. We want to hear comforting things, and do not want to be challenged to change. In the illuminative stage, however, the Lord's Day is a time of profound worship — a time to spend with God and to abstain from any work that distracts from authentically consecrating Sunday as a precious day of love of God and love of neighbor. We seek comfort, but one also seeks to be challenged to grow.

The fourth commandment demands the authentic honoring of mother and father.[209] In the purgative stage this is seen primarily in terms of obedience and respect. On the part of the parents, the obligation is viewed primarily in terms of the education and rearing of children in an emotionally and spiritually stable home. In the illuminative stage, there is a much deeper realization of the implications of this fourth commandment. The son or daughter in the illuminative stage is acutely aware of the importance of gratitude and the repaying of love with love. In this stage, often the most precious love given, the most precious respect or honor, is in calling parents to live a holy life when they are not. Parents in the illuminative stage are made acutely aware of the priority of nourishing the spiritual needs of their children. It is a time for encouraging a holy vocation and a time of fostering the living out of a virtuous life.

The fifth commandment is an affirmation of the dignity of life, of not murdering.[210] In the purgative stage there is a clear

---

[208] Cf. CCC 2168-2188.
[209] Cf. CCC 2197-2246.
[210] Cf. CCC 2258-2317.

awareness of the horror of unjust wars, direct abortions, intentional euthanasia and the general recognition that all life is sacred from conception to natural death.

The deep implications of the dignity of the person however are often not fully grasped at this stage. In the illuminative stage one is enlightened as to the more profound reasons for this commandment. For example, direct abortion is seen as the blatant killing of the image and likeness of God, contraception is seen as an affront to God's gift of co-creation, intentional euthanasia is seen as the rejecting of the redemptive value of suffering, and suicide is seen as an act of violence against justice, hope, and love.

The sixth commandment is a command that demands fidelity.[211] In the purgative stage the person is aware of most acts that are an affront to the dignity of chastity, such as adultery, fornication, polygamy, open or free marriages, homosexual and bisexual acts, masturbation, pornography, and divorce. What is often unperceived in the purgative stage, and which needs enlightenment, is the reasoning behind these commands. A person fails to see that the indissolubility of marriage is based on the indissoluble bond between Christ and his Church and that chastity involves the authentic sexual integration within a person that makes him or her authentically human, authentically at peace.

The seventh commandment is a prohibition against stealing.[212] It is most often seen in the purgative stage in a limited manner. Injustice and lack of charity become more and more prominently seen at this stage. Alms for the poor become an easy act to perform in response to God's will (Lk 17:19-31; Mt 25:45). What is still in need of enlightenment is the recognition that stealing is just as serious or perhaps more serious when it is manifested in the mistreatment of workers (e.g., an unfair wage, lack of health

---

[211] Cf. CCC 2331-2391.
[212] Cf. CCC 2401-2449.

benefits, and a lack of a decent pension plan), the exploitation of the world's resources, the lack of appreciation for the common good of society, and the redemptive nature of work.

The eighth commandment is a prohibition against bearing false witness against our neighbor.[213] In the early stages of the spiritual journey there is a pretty good grasp of the transgressions against this commandment. We are aware of lying, of being duplicitous, double-faced, disparaging, of being a hypocrite. We are aware of tricks that involve dissimulation; that is, hiding under a false appearance. We are aware of the betrayal of another's confidences and the destruction of another's character by calumny or character assassination. But it is only in the more enlightened stages of the spiritual life that we realize the true damage that we have done to another in the breaking of the eighth commandment. How many people have put an end to their lives because of the slanderous destruction of their reputation?

The ninth commandment is a prohibition against coveting one's neighbor's wife.[214] In the early stages this is perceived as respecting our neighbor as an act of decency and modesty. It is seen as the curbing of our lust and the redirecting of that energy in a more appropriate way. As we progress in the spiritual life, this commandment makes demands on not only the external following of the requirements of the commandment but also on the internal living and embracing of that commandment — that is, in purity of heart, intention and vision (cf. Mt 5:28). As the cenobitic monk, Pseudo-Macarius explains, our "inner [being] regards all with a pure eye."[215]

The tenth commandment is a call to avoid coveting another's goods.[216] For most Christians this is associated with a person who

---

[213] Cf. CCC 2464-2499.
[214] Cf. CCC 2514-2527.
[215] *Fifty Spiritual Homilies of St. Macarius the Great*, Homily VIII, n. 6.
[216] Cf. CCC 2534-2550.

The Illuminative Stage

avoids avarice and envy and all immoderate desires. As we progress this initial understanding is enlightened by the desire for detachment (cf. Gal 5:24) and the tremendous thirst for God alone (cf. Jn 4:14).

The ten commandments become more and more absorbed in the illuminative stage into the reality of authentic love. We begin to experience and live out the dimensions of love to such an extent that the commandments that are written in the core of our being become more natural to our nature. In the subsequent stages, particularly in the unitive stage, the highest level of spirituality, the ten commandments are completely fulfilled in the commandment of love, which not only fulfills the ten commandments but also enlightens their full implications.

Discernment of Spirits[217]

> Beware of false prophets, who come to you in sheep's clothing but inwardly are ravenous wolves (Mt 7:15).

The discernment of spirits is guided by acquired and infused prudence and the gift of counsel. In the purgative stage, the spirit of the world or nature predominates. In the illuminative stage, the Spirit of God takes a hold of a person's spiritual journey. The spirit of the devil is identifiable and slowly being destroyed.

The Spirit of the Devil

The spirit of the devil is marked by pride, discouragement, despair, scrupulosity, boasting, dissension, hatreds, false humility, presumption, fear of correction, self-infatuation, bitter zeal,

---

[217] Cf. Ignatius, *Spiritual Exercises*, 4th week.

forgetfulness of God, lack of obedience, and an intense dislike for mortification. All that is contrary to the honor and glory of God is found in the influences of the devil.

The Spirit of the World

The spirit of the world bears a lot in common with the spirit of the devil. However, the spirit of the world does not bear the extreme evil that is indicative of the ways of the devil. In this phase, a person has very little regard for the infused virtues of faith, hope, and love. In this stage they are pleasure and self-oriented, easily irritated and discouraged and indifferent to the glory and honor of God as well as to the love of God and the love of neighbor. There is no zeal in such a person. Tepidity, mediocrity, and false moderation are indicative of a person's spiritual life. People influenced by the spirit of the world (or nature) are people who are more social workers than disciples. They are the ones who at the first sign of difficulty in the spiritual life, abandon it, and go to their former way of life.

The Spirit of God

> But the fruit of the Spirit is love, joy, peace, patience, kindness, goodness, faithfulness, gentleness, self-control; against such there is no law. And those who belong to Christ Jesus have crucified the flesh with its passions and desires (Gal 5:22-24).

All that is of the Spirit of God is directed toward the honor and glory of God. Those who live in this manner bear the marks of faith, hope, and love. They are people of true, authentic humility bearing profound self-knowledge and a zeal for God. They are a people marked by interior joy and forgetfulness of self. They embrace suffering, the sweetness of the cross, and mortification.

The Illuminative Stage

They have no regard for the world's standards of success or the world's scorn.

Authentic mortification takes place in those embraced with the Spirit of God. That which is of the Spirit of God in terms of mortification is always marked by respect for the body as the temple of God. Mortification that flows from the grace of God is moderated by discretion and obedience. A person engaged in mortification does not seek to attract attention, and he or she does not seek to damage his or her health. Rather, authentic mortification is directed toward purifying the heart and the will for the honor and glory of God.

The illuminative stage is exemplified by a person's ability to discern the spirits and to persevere in the Spirit of God. As St. John Climacus states:

> It is characteristic of the [profoundly holy] that they always know whether a thought comes from within themselves, or from God, or from the demons…. The eyes of the heart are enlightened by discernment to things seen and unseen….[218]

Perceiving Christ in Others

Carryll Houselander, while traveling on a crowded underground train during rush hour in London, experienced this profound sense of seeing all people as Christs.

> I was in an underground train, a crowded train in which all sorts of people jolted together, sitting and strap-hanging — workers of every description going home at the end of the day. Quite suddenly I saw with my mind, but as

---

[218] *John Climacus: The Ladder of Divine Ascent*, 255.

vividly as a wonderful picture, Christ in them all. But I saw more than that; not only was Christ in every one of them, living in them, dying in them, rejoicing in them, sorrowing in them — but because He was in them, and because they were here, the whole world was here too, here in this underground train; not only the world as it was at that moment, not only the people in all the countries of the world, but all those people who had lived in the past, and all those yet to come. I came out into the street and walked for a long time in the crowds. It was the same here, on every side, in every passerby, everywhere — Christ.[219]

This sense of the everywhere of Christ is expressed in a prayer ascribed to St. Patrick:

Christ be with me, Christ within me, Christ behind me, Christ before me, Christ beside me, Christ to win me, Christ to comfort me and restore me, Christ beneath me, Christ above me, Christ in the hearts of all that love me, Christ in the mouth of friend and stranger.

Patrick sought to experience a world engulfed in Christ.

Prayer in the Illuminative Stage — Meditation to Contemplation

What began in the passive purification of the senses continues more profoundly in the illuminative stage of spirituality. Meditation is being transformed into contemplation. It slowly becomes more simplified to such an extent that the various experiences and acts involved in meditation begin to fuse into a single act. Our core being has been made docile to the workings of the Holy Spirit and our experience of prayer is raised to that of contemplation.

The Illuminative Stage

Contemplation is a mutual sharing among friends, a mutual presence, an inter-indwelling, a gaze on the guest within (cf. 1 Jn 4:16).[219][220] It is a pure, supernatural gift, an inflaming of love.[221] The Song of Songs in the Scriptures is the perfect analogy for the experience that occurs in the silence of the soul in contemplation. One who experiences contemplation is transformed into a person of great virtue, into a person of profound works (Mt 7:20). The following are key aspects of the fruits of contemplation:[222]

- Peace, quietude, calm, repose, serenity, and rest beyond all understanding (cf. Ph 4:4-7).
- A knowledge of realities that transcend the natural means of knowing.
- A deepening, wounding, inflaming, engulfing, inflowing, longing love that is caused by God's self-communicating triune nature.
- Transformation into the image and likeness of God.

Contemplation is an act of the intellect that is superior to reasoning. It is a simple glance at truth, which springs from love. It is an act that proceeds from faith and is enlightened by the gifts of the Holy Spirit, especially wisdom and understanding. In the beginning, contemplation can be prepared for by the reading of Sacred Scripture, meditation, prayers of petitions, and centering prayer. This helps to prepare us to experience contemplation. With time, however, these preparatory acts will not be necessary.[223] At this stage, God himself will teach and refresh the core of our be-

---

[219] Caryll Houselander, *A Rocking-Horse Catholic* (New York: Sheed and Ward, 1955), 137-138.
[220] *Life*, Ch. 8, no. 5 and Ch. 10, no. 1; *Way*, Ch. 27.
[221] *Way*, Ch. 23, no. 5; Ch. 24, nos. 7-8; Ch. 39, no. 23.
[222] *Way*, Ch. 27, no. 4; *Ascent*, Bk. II, Chs. 12-15; *Dark Night*, Bk. I, no. 1, and Chs. 5, 8-13, 17; *Spiritual Canticle*, St. 39, no. 12.
[223] ST IIa IIae, q. 180, a. 3, 4, 6, 7 ad 1um; IIa IIae, q. 8, a. 1, 2, 4, 6, 7; q. 45, a. 1, 2, 5, 6.

ing without meditation or any active effort.[224] Contemplation thus becomes, in the words of St. John of the Cross, the "science of love," which is an infused knowledge of God.[225]

Degrees of Prayer in the Illuminative Stage

St. Teresa of Avila and St. John of the Cross describe most profoundly the various degrees of prayer in the illuminative way:[226]

1) The discursive meditations that survive the passive purification of the senses continue to transform us as we continue to grow in the virtues. As we progress in the spiritual journey, meditation will give way to initial infused contemplation.

   a) St. John of the Cross sets a threefold guideline in determining when we should progress from meditation to contemplation. First, we should experience no comfort in the imagination or the senses in our attempts at meditation. Second, the memory that lingers on in prayer is one that is filled with anxiety, with a sense that makes us feel that we are going backwards or not serving God. Finally, we are consciously aware of an inability to meditate or engage in reflections, or to excite our imagination.[227]

2) The second degree of prayer in the illuminative way can be pictured as a pump or water-wheel that draws up water. This second degree requires much less effort and yields much more water, much more spiritual fruit. This is the stage of prayer that Teresa calls the "prayer of quiet."[228] It is that level of

---

[224] *Dark Night*, Bk. I, Ch. 14.
[225] *Dark Night*, Bk. II, Ch. 18.
[226] Cf. *Life*, Chs. 11-19.
[227] *Dark Night*, Bk. I, Ch. 9.
[228] *Life*, 14f.

The Illuminative Stage

prayer where the will is seized and held.[229] This "prayer of quiet" has three distinct phases: In the first phase, our will experiences a sweet and loving sense of being absorbed by God. In the second phase we experience a sense of quiet tranquility because the will is now not only absorbed by God but it is now captivated by God. In the third phase, the will is still captivated and our ability to understand what is happening to our soul is no longer perceivable. The virtues flower, and the soul is docile in responding to the gift of piety. Yet, in this "prayer of quiet" we are still susceptible to distractions in prayer, for the intellect, the memory and the imagination still continue to enter into our prayer experience.[230] Centering prayer becomes very good at this stage of the spiritual journey.

3) The third degree in the prayer life in the illuminative stage can be described in a way similar to a person who irrigates his or her garden with running water. Another image used is that of water overflowing a riverbank and washing up onto a garden. This is the type of prayer that is often referred to as the "prayer of simple union." God's self-communicating presence at this stage is such that the interior faculties at the core of our being are now put to sleep. It is a time where our intellect is seized and held, and it is a time when our exterior senses and imagination "fall asleep." It is often an ecstatic state.[231] God is the object of all the activities of the inner core of our being. There is no longer any wandering. Our will, thought, imagination and memory are captivated and absorbed by God. All things are calmed. There is no more restlessness.[232]

---

[229] *Interior Castle*, 5th mansion, Ch. 1.
[230] *Life*, Chs. 14 and 17; *Interior Castle*, 4th mansion, Ch. 2.
[231] *Interior Castle*, 5th mansion, Ch. 1.
[232] *Life*, Ch. 18f.

4) There is a fourth degree of prayer in the life of a person that is called the "prayer of union." It is, however, that degree of prayer that is reserved to those who reach the highest stage of the spiritual journey, the unitive stage. It is the prayer of the mystics.[233] This is the stage in the spiritual journey that is marked by the prayer of "transforming union" or "mystical union."[234] It is like a gentle, abundant rainfall that nourishes a garden completely. The person does nothing to water the garden. It is all God's doing.[235] This reality is described by St. Bernard of Clairvaux in his *Sermon 74*:

> I remember afterwards that he had been with me; sometimes I had a presentiment that he would come, but I was never conscious of his coming or his going. And where he comes from when he visits my soul, and where he goes, and by what means he enters and goes out, I admit that I do not know even now.... The coming of the Word was not perceptible to my eyes, for he has not color; nor to the ears, for there was no sound; nor yet to my nostrils, for he mingles with the mind, not the air; he has not acted upon the air, but created it. His coming was not tasted by the mouth, for there was not eating or drinking, nor could he be known by the sense of touch, for he is not tangible. How then did he enter? Perhaps he did not enter because he does not come from outside? He is not one of the things which exist outside us. Yet he does not come from within me, for he is good, and I know there is no good in me. I have ascended to the highest in me, and look! the word is towering above that. In my curiosity I have descended

---

[233] Cf. *Life*, Ch. 18f.
[234] *Interior Castle*, 7th mansion, Ch. 3.
[235] *Life*, Ch. 11, no. 7.

The Illuminative Stage

to explore my lowest depths, yet I found him even deeper. If I look outside myself, I saw him stretching beyond the furthest I could see; and if I looked within, he was yet further within. Then I knew the truth of what I had read, "in him we live and move and have our being." And blessed is the man in whom he has his being, who lives for him and is moved by him.[236]

The Our Father[237]

[This] prayer, the Our Father, contains the fullness of perfection. It was the Lord Himself who gave it to us as both an example and a rule.... It lifts them up to that prayer of fire known to so few. It lifts them up, rather, to that ineffable prayer which rises above all human consciousness with no voice sounding, no tongue moving, no words uttered. The soul lights up with heavenly illumination and no longer employs constricted, human speech.[238]

St. John Cassian

In the *Our Father* Jesus teaches us how to pray. Since he experienced all things we experience, except sin, he knows well our needs (cf. Heb 4:15). Jesus in the *Our Father* teaches us the summary of the whole Gospel, the summary of what new life in God is all about. In this prayer we are empowered by the Spirit to cry out "Abba," "Father" (cf. Jn 6:63; Gal 4:6)! In the Lord's Prayer we are brought into the presence of the Father, of the Trinity. In

---

[236] *Bernard of Clairvaux: On the Song of Songs IV*, trans. Kilian Walsh, O.C.S.O. (Kalamazoo: Cistercian Publications, 1980), Sermon 74.
[237] See CCC 2777-2856.
[238] *John Cassian: Conferences*, Trans. Colm Luibheid (Mahwah: Paulist Press, 1985), Conference 9, n. 25.

the *Our Father* we enter a prayer of "straightforward simplicity, filial trust, joyous assurance, humble boldness, and certainty of being loved"[239] (cf. Eph 3:12; Heb 3:6; 4:16; 10:19; 1 Jn 2:28; 3:21; 5:14). As a prayer the *Our Father* reveals the Father and reveals our own innermost being: It enlightens us to the Father and to our core self.

Our Father

By saying "Our Father" we are saying that we are entering a relationship. He is our God and we are his people (cf. Jn 1:17; Ho 2:21-22; 6:1-6). We accept the reality that we have also entered a relationship that implies not individualism but a sense of communion, of membership. We are members of God's Body, the Church, the community of faith (cf. Ac 4:32; Jn 11:52). We recognize that the communion between the three Persons of the Trinity must be modeled by God's people, who were and are created in the image and likeness of God. Prayer is always therefore a community-oriented experience. Even in what appears to be private prayer, we are in prayer with the unknown and with the angels and saints.

Who art in heaven

> "Our Father who art in heaven" is rightly understood to mean that God is in the hearts of the just, as in his holy temple. At the same time, it means that those who pray should desire the one they invoke to dwell in them.[240]
>
> *St. Augustine*

---

[239] CCC 2778.
[240] St. Augustine, *De serm. Dom. in monte* 2, 5, 18: PL 34, 1277.

The phrase "who art in heaven" is not primarily a reference to a place because heaven is not a "place" as commonly understood. Heaven is a place in the sense that it is a dimension beyond space and time: Heaven is another dimension of reality. Consequently the phrase, used in the context of this prayer, is primarily a reference to God's majesty and his presence in the hearts of the just. Heaven, "the Father's house, is the true homeland toward which we are heading and to which, already, we belong."[241]

Hallowed be thy name

The phrase "Hallowed be thy name" is a phrase that conjures up the holiness, preciousness, and majesty of God (cf. Ps 8:5; Is 6:3). It reminds us that God is worthy of all praise and thanksgiving (cf. Ps 111:9; Lk 1:49).

Thy Kingdom Come

God's kingdom became present in the first coming and will find its fulfillment in the second coming (cf. Tt 2:13). As followers of Christ we are called to help bring about the fulfillment of this kingdom. We are called upon to help build the kingdom of God here on earth, a kingdom of love.

Thy will be done on earth as it is in heaven

This phrase is an affirmation that
1) we are called to be saved and come to the truth (cf. 1 Tm 2:3-4; 2 P 3:9; Mt 18:14).
2) we must love one another (Jn 13:34; cf. 1 Jn 3; 4; Lk 10: 25-37).

---

[241] CCC 2802.

3) we must do all things according to God's will (Eph 1:9-11).
4) we are called to imitate Christ in his obedience and surrendering to the Father's will (Heb 10:7; Lk 22:42; Jn 4:34; 5:30; 6:38; 8:29; Gal 1:4).

Give us this day our daily bread

This statement is an expression of God's goodness, a goodness that transcends all other goodness. The "Our" reminds us that we are members of a community, a community built upon the foundation of solidarity. It is a call in trust and in a spirit of surrender to God. It is a call for God to meet our personal and our community's material and spiritual needs. It is a call to responsibility and justice (cf. Lk 16:19-31; Mt 25:31-46).

Another aspect of this phrase reminds us of the most important food of all, the Word of God and the Eucharist, the Body, Blood, Soul and Divinity of Christ. Without this food, Christian life is impossible, for it is the food of immortality. As St. Augustine and St. Peter Chrysologus point out, respectively:

> The Eucharist is our daily bread. The power belonging to this divine food makes it a bond of union. Its effect is then understood as unity, so that, gathered into his Body and made members of him, we may become what we receive.... This also is our daily bread: the readings you hear each day in church and the hymns you hear and sing. All these are necessities for our pilgrimage.[242]
>
> The Father in heaven urges us, as children of heaven, to ask for the bread of heaven. [Christ] himself is the bread who, sown in the Virgin, raised up in the flesh, kneaded

---

[242] St. Augustine, *Sermo* 57, 7: PL 38, 389.

in the Passion, baked in the oven of the tomb, reserved in churches, brought to altars, furnishes the faithful each day with food from heaven.[243]

And forgive us our trespasses as we forgive those who trespass against us

Love of God and love of neighbor are one reality. Any authentic love of God implies the love of neighbor, and any authentic love of neighbor implies an authentic love of God. How can we love God if we do not love our neighbor (cf. 1 Jn 4:20; Mt 5: 43-44; 6:14-15; 5:23-24; 18:23-35; Mk 11:25)? How can we ask for God's forgiveness if we are unwilling to forgive those whom God loves?

And lead us not into temptation

This petition is a call to be set free from the snares of evil. The spirit of discernment and strength become intrinsic to this petition. The Spirit guides us to discern between temptations, trials and tribulations that are for our personal growth in the life of God (cf. Lk 8:13-15; Ac 14:22; Rm 5:3-5; 2 Tm 3:12) and those temptations, trials and tribulations that lead to sin and death (cf. Jm 1:14-15). We discern the difference between being tempted (which is not sinful and in fact can lead to great spiritual growth) and consenting to temptation. The Spirit helps us to discern and unmask the lies behind the temptations (cf. Gn 3:6) and helps us to persevere through them to become strong in God (cf. 1 Cor 10:13; Rv 16:15).

---

[243] St. Peter Chrysologus, *Sermo* 67: PL 52, 392; cf. Jn 6:51.

But deliver us from evil

This is a petition that asks for protection from the cunning of the devil (cf. Jn 17:15). The devil seeks to distort God's providential plan and seeks to destroy people in the process under the guise of doing good for them (cf. Jn 8:44; Rv 12:9). We find confidence in this petition in that just as we have been delivered from evil in the past, we will be delivered from the evil one in the present and in the future if we persevere in the spiritual battle.

> The Lord who has taken away your sin and pardoned your faults also protects you and keeps you from the wiles of your adversary the devil, so that the enemy, who is accustomed to leading into sin, may not surprise you. One who entrusts himself to God does not dread the devil. "If God is for us, who is against us?"[244]   *St. Ambrose*

---

[244] St. Ambrose, *De Sacr.* 5, 4, 30: PL 16, 454; cf. Rm 8:31.

7

The Second Dark Night
The Passive Purification of the Spirit
(or Passive Purification of the Spiritual Soul)

> For a short time he allows us to taste how sweet he is, and before our taste is satisfied he withdraws; and it is in this way, by flying above us with wings outspread, that he encourages us to fly and says in effect: See now, you have had a little taste of how sweet and delightful I am, but if you wish to have your fill of this sweetness, hasten after me, drawn by my sweet-smelling perfumes, lift up your heart to where I am at the right hand of God the Father. There you will see me not darkly in a mirror but face to face, and "your heart's joy will be complete and no one shall take this joy away from you"....[245]
>
> *Guigo II*

At the end of the illuminative stage of the spiritual life, we encounter the second *dark night*, the passive purification of the spirit. The passive purification of the spirit is a "mystical death" to self that takes place within us.

During the illuminative stage God has given us, in a sense, a rest from the pain of the first *dark night*, the purification of the

---
[245] *Guigo II: The Ladder of Monks*, quoted in Egan, 211.

senses. Now God desires to complete the purification that began in the very beginning of the spiritual journey. At this level of the spiritual journey we are saints who are still in need of some fine-tuning.

In the passive purification of the senses that we often experience as beginners, we are purified of sensible consolations that we might find ourselves being excessively attached to. In the passive purification of the spirit we are being divested of any remaining stains of superficial knowledge in matters pertaining to God. The remaining defects in the will and the intellect, and the remaining weaknesses of intellectual and spiritual pride still need to be conquered. In the *dark night of the senses* the main battle that took place was over temptations against chastity and patience. In the *dark night of the spirit*, the main battle is over the temptations against faith and hope.

God at this stage is stripping us to the core. Every aspect of our being, particularly our ways of thinking and praying, are being made anew. At this stage we feel deprived of God's divine illumination, his divine light. Darkness appears. We experience a pain worse than martyrdom. The suffering at this stage is the ultimate purifier. As St. John of the Cross puts it,

> God divests the faculties, affections, and senses, both spiritual and sensory, interior and exterior. He leaves the intellect in darkness, the will in aridity, the memory in emptiness, and the affections in supreme affliction, bitterness, and anguish by depriving the soul of the feeling and satisfaction it previously obtained from spiritual blessings.[246]

This is a time of great sadness. "My God, my God, why have you forsaken me?" is the cry of the person in this predicament. We

---

[246] *Dark Night*, Bk. II, Ch. 3, 3.

feel alone, abandoned, lost, no longer loved, on the verge of despair. We feel as if we were being ripped apart, torn down. We become painfully aware of our wretchedness and our need for God. The only thing that keeps us going is the grace-driven hunger for God and the desire of being purified for him. The call is to walk in pure faith, in pure hope, and in pure love, which is pure darkness to our faculties.[247]

Why the Suffering? Why the Darkness?

> Truly, truly, I say to you, unless a grain of wheat falls into the earth and dies, it remains alone; but if it dies, it bears much fruit. He who loves his life loses it, and he who hates his life in this world will keep it for eternal life (Jn 12:24-25).

At this stage of the spiritual journey we enter into darkness not because of a lack of God's light, but because of an excess of God's divine light, his divine presence. The divine presence is so powerful that it transcends our capacity to contain it. This blindness can be compared to looking into the sun directly. The sun is so bright that it blinds the sight.[248]

This divine light inevitably causes suffering, for its goal is to purify the soul of all that is not for the honor and glory of God. It is a suffering caused by the purification of any impurities still left in the core of our being. A purifying light, a spiritual fire is ridding our inner being of all its stains, of all that is contrary to love, faith and hope, of all aspects of ignorance, self-infatuation, half-truths, inordinate desires for consolations, and imperfections of any kind. It is an earthly purgatory. The cleansing words of the

---
[247] *Dark Night*, Bk. II, Chs. 4; 5; 8f.
[248] *Dark Night*, Chs. 5 and 12.

Scriptures come alive here: "The Lord our God is a devouring fire..." (Dt 4:24). "From on high he sent fire; into my bones he made it descend..." (Lm 1:13). "[Like] gold in a furnace he tried [me], and like a sacrificial burnt offering he accepted [me]" (Ws 3:6).[249]

In this purifying fire of grace, God is healing our inner being. He is transforming us into Christ by detaching us of all so that all we can see is God himself. We are being prepared for intimacy with God, for a "mystical death," a death to self and a new birth in the splendor of God. We are becoming nothing so that we can become everything!

What must we do to get through this stage?

We must heed the words of St. John of the Cross: "God teaches the soul secretly and instructs it in the perfection of love without its doing anything or understanding how this happens."[250] Because of this reality we must be completely abandoned to the divine will and to divine providence (Rm 4:18).[251] We must pray for perseverance, and live by faith, hope and love. We must carry our cross and unite ourselves with Christ's passion (cf. Rm 1:17). We must abandon ourselves to God's mercy and pray for the intercession of the saints, and particularly the intercession of the Blessed Mother. We must cry out in the words of the Psalmist, "Thou art holy, enthroned on the praises of Israel. In thee our fathers trusted; they trusted and thou didst deliver them" (Ps 22:3-4).

---

[249] *Dark Night*, Chs. 5, 10, and 12; *Treatise*, Bk. II, Ch. 1.
[250] *Dark Night*, Bk. II, Ch. 5, 1.
[251] *Treatise*, Bk. IX, Chs. 3-6; 12-16.

The Second Dark Night

The Precious Outcome of the Burning Flame

The theological virtues of faith, hope, and love, with the help of the Spirit's gifts of understanding, knowledge, and piety are elevated to heights previously unknown. Because of this reality, we become a new creation in Christ. There are no longer any vestiges of spiritual and intellectual pride, no vestiges of selfish attraction to our own way of seeing, feeling, and willing, and no vestiges of rudeness, impatience, bitter zeal, jealousy, slander, discord, delusions, or unconscious egoism.

Those who come out of the *dark night of the spirit* have entered the unitive stage of spirituality. They have become an open treasure chest to God's love and are living in a new realm. They seek to be nothing, so that God may be everything, and by so seeking nothing they become everything. They seek to love God for simply being God, as opposed to loving God for what he can give. Love truly becomes as strong as death for such persons (Song of Songs 8:6). They begin to see the world the way Christ sees the world; that is, to see the world the way the world truly is. Guided by the gifts of knowledge and understanding, they delve into the mysteries of God that transcend the limits of human reason.[252]

After a long journey in this *dark night* we can say with St. Thérèse of Lisieux:

> [In] the crucible of trials from within and without, my soul has been refined, and I can raise my head like a flower after a storm and see how the words of the Psalm have been fulfilled in my case: "The Lord is my Shepherd and I shall want nothing."[253]

---

[252] Cf. *Dark Night*, Bk. II, Chs. 2, 5, 9; ST IIa IIae, q. 8, a. 1, 8.
[253] St. Thérèse, *Story of a Soul*, 3.

8

The Unitive Stage
A Taste of Heaven

> There is no other path than through the burning love of the crucified.... For no one is in any way disposed for divine contemplation that leads to mystical ecstasy unless like Daniel he is a man of desires (Dn 9:23).[254]
>
> *St. Bonaventure*

The unitive stage of spirituality is the realm where the mystics live. This is the stage where a new transformation has taken place within the very core of the person. A new life begins here, a life like nothing ever before, a life that will only be surpassed in its bliss by the experience of heaven itself.

It is a stage where one has entered the ultimate sphere of being dissolved in God.[255] It is a realm where the Spirit's gifts of wisdom, understanding, counsel, fortitude, knowledge, piety, wonder and awe come to their fullest expression. It is where the fruits of the Spirit such as charity, joy, peace, patience, benignity, goodness, mildness, faith, modesty, and chastity are enjoyed. It is where the capital sins of pride, covetousness, lust, anger, gluttony, envy, and sloth are non-existent.

---

[254] Bonaventure, *The Soul's Journey into God*, trans. Evert Cousins (Mahwah: Paulist Press, 1979), n. 5.
[255] Cf. ST IIa IIae, q. 24, a. 9.

The unitive stage is the stage of heroes. It is the stage where heroic virtue is lived out in its ultimate expression.[256]

The Heroic Theological Virtues

Faith

> I am never afraid. I am doing my work with Jesus, I'm doing it for Jesus, I'm doing it to Jesus, and therefore the results are His, not mine. If you need a guide, you only have to look to Jesus. You have to surrender to Him and rely on Him completely. When you do this, all doubt is dispelled and you are filled with conviction.[257]
>
> *Mother Teresa*

Faith at this stage in the spiritual journey is exemplified by its penetration, firmness, and promptness. A person of such profound faith is a person capable of penetrating the deepest mysteries of divine revelation. Such a person lives life contemplating all things in light of God's will. Reality is seen the way it really, authentically is: it is seen the way God sees it. Because of this deep penetration and firmness of faith, a person at this level of faith adheres not only to the great mysteries of the faith, but also to the most obscure aspects. There are no "cafeteria" Catholics at this stage of the faith. Promptness in decisions regarding one's eternal destiny and the eternal destiny of others becomes paramount. The great insight acquired at this level of life makes the rejection of errors easy, for all that is not of God screams emptiness. A person in the unitive stage of spirituality can be said to have a contemplative faith.[258]

---

[256] Cf. ST Ia IIae, q. 61, a. 5, q. 69.
[257] *Mother Teresa: A Simple Path*, compiled by Lucinda Vardey (New York: Ballantine Books, 1995), 44.
[258] Cf. ST IIa IIae, q. 8, a. 1, 3.

Hope

> The basic attitude of hope, on the one hand, encourages the Christian not to lose sight of the final goal which gives meaning and value to life; and on the other hand, [it] offers solid and profound reasons for a daily commitment to God's plan.[259]
> *Pope John Paul II*

There is a complete surrendering to God's will and his providence at this level of hope. Aided by the Spirit's gift of wisdom a person can live out the heroic life of hope in such a way that all the trials and tribulations of life are responded to with the words, "I can do all things in him who strengthens me" (Ph 4:13) and firmly say: "If God is for us, who can be against us?" (Rm 8:31). Trust in God at this plateau is unequalled. The words of Jesus become reality: "Ask, and it will be given you; seek, and you will find; knock, and it will be opened to you. For every one who asks receives, and he who seeks finds, and to him who knocks it will be opened" (Lk 11:9-10).

At this plateau in the spiritual life, hope becomes transformed into a sense of invisible trust, abandonment, and firmness in our eternal destiny, life with God in heaven. While heaven is never assured on this earthly journey, for God's love always requires a response, the sense of our eternal destiny attains a firmness that makes turning away from God almost impossible. In a sense, we feel that we have reached the *point of no return*, that to turn back would be a loss of such catastrophic proportions that we would cease to exist.

---

[259] John Paul II, *Celebrate 2000*, 81.

Love

> You possess a wonderful and noble goal: to try to find ways of putting into practice your love for God and for your neighbor. Faith in action is love, and love in action is service. By transforming faith into living acts of love, we put ourselves in contact with God himself, with Jesus our Lord.[260]
> Mother Teresa

Love of God and love of neighbor become experienced beyond anything that has ever been experienced before. We love God completely for just being God. No more is there a longing for what I can get from God or what I can get from my neighbor by loving him or her. We love God completely for just being God. We love our neighbor for simply being the image of God. As Evagrius Ponticus, the Desert Father mentions, "Happy is the... [person] who considers all [people] as god — after God."[261]

At this stage the love of God and the love of neighbor become for all practical purposes a single reality. To authentically love God we need to authentically love our neighbor and to authentically love our neighbor we have to authentically love God.

At this stage of love we grasp the mystery of the intimacy of Christ's human will with his divine will. The human will of Jesus was in complete conformity with his divine will. One who experiences the heights of heroic love experiences a taste of this mystery of wills. While it is true that we do not have two wills, nor two natures like the God-man Jesus Christ, our single, human will and God's will can become, because of love, one. While God's nature and the nature of the human spiritual person are distinct realities, that human spiritual person can grow in response to God's

---

[260] Mother Teresa, *One Heart Full of Love*, 1.
[261] Evagrius Ponticus, *The 153 Chapters on Prayer*, 123, in Harvey Egan, *An Anthology of Mysticism* (Collegeville: The Liturgical Press, 1991), 52.

The Unitive Stage

grace to such a level of love that that person's every desire and action can be conformed with God's. Two truly become spiritually one. We truly become, as the Fathers of the Church so often echoed, *divinized*.

Consequently, love of the cross reaches its apex in the unitive stage of love, for within the cross is the mystery of Christ's love.

> Let's fix our eyes on the cross. What do we see? We see his head bent down to kiss us. Look at his hands. They say, "I love you!" We see his arms stretched out on the cross as if to embrace us. We see his heart opened wide to receive us. That is the cross, which is represented by the crucifix that most of us have in our homes. Each time we glance at it, it should help us to fall in love with Christ. It should help us to love him with sincerity of heart. What greater love is there than God's love for each of us? ....[262]

> Suffering — pain, humiliation, sickness and failure is but a kiss of Jesus. Suffering is a gift of God, a gift that makes us most Christ-like. People must not accept suffering as a punishment.... Any who imitate Jesus to the full must also share in his passion. Suffering is meant to purify, to sanctify, to make us Christ-like.[263]   *Mother Teresa*

The Heroic Moral Virtues

Humility

> Humility is nothing but truth. If we are humble, nothing will touch us — neither praise nor contempt — for we know what we are.... Knowing ourselves puts us in our

---
[262] Mother Teresa, *One Heart Full of Love*, 95.
[263] Mother Teresa, *Words to Love By...* (New York: Walker and Company, 1983), 61-67.

rightful places. This knowing is necessary for love because the knowledge of God yields love, and self-knowledge yields humility.[264] *Mother Teresa*

In the unitive stage humility is experienced as never before. Humility is essentially self-knowledge. To know ourselves the way we truly are is what humility is all about. We now see ourselves the way God sees us. Self-knowledge at this stage is now uncluttered by inordinate self-infatuation. It is uncluttered from all things that hinder self-knowledge and the powerful imitation of Christ and the majesty of God reflected in all creatures.[265]

Humility finds its greatest expression at this stage in our ability to take ridicule, abasement, and humiliation without any concern for our own self. We see these assaults as opportunities to share in the cross of Jesus Christ.

This stage is a period of extraordinary modesty. There is no conceit or vanity in us.

Meekness

"Blessed are the meek, for they shall inherit the earth" (Mt 5:5). Those who are meek are patient and gentle. This is the stage of our walk in grace that leads to perfect self-mastery — as perfect as is possible on this earthly journey. We do not return evil with evil. We dominate our passions, particularly the passion of unjustified anger. We find no disturbance in being injured; rather, we experience great empathy and compassion for the one doing the injuring.[266] St. Francis of Assisi exemplified the reality of this heroic virtue in his legendary prayer of gentleness:

---

[264] Mother Teresa, *Heart of Joy*, 133.
[265] Cf. ST IIa IIae, q. 160, a. 1, 2; q. 161, a. 1, 3, 6 ad 3um.
[266] Cf. ST IIa IIae, q. 157, a. 1, 2, 4.

The Unitive Stage

> Lord, make me an instrument of your peace.
> Where there is hatred, let me sow love.
> Where there is injury, pardon.
> Where there is doubt, faith.
> Where there is despair, hope.
> Where there is darkness, light.
> Where there is sadness, joy.
> O Divine Master,
> grant that I may not so much seek
> to be consoled as to console;
> to be understood as to understand;
> to be loved as to love.
> For it is in giving that we receive;
> it is in pardoning that we are pardoned;
> and it is in dying that we are born to eternal life.

Fortitude

> There are always souls to enlighten, sinners to pardon, tears to dry, disappointments to console, sick to encourage, children and youngsters to guide. There is, there ever shall be, [people] to love and save, in Christ's name! This is your vocation; it ought to make you happy and courageous.[267] *Pope John Paul II*

Here the moral virtue of fortitude or courage is magnified by the Spirit's gift of fortitude. At this stage of our life we are able to pursue in an extraordinary way that which is very difficult to do but which is very necessary to do. Fear, danger, fatigue, criticism, and so forth, are dominated and mastered. All that we undertake is accomplished with great courage, from the simplest task to the most difficult.

---

[267] John Paul II, *Prayers and Devotions* (New York: Viking, 1994), 299.

Magnanimity

Closely associated with the gift of fortitude is the gift of magnanimity — the ability to endure trials for extended periods of time with patience and courage. Martyrdom is the quintessential expression of this grace-elevated virtue.[268] In the spiritual diaries of St. John de Brebeuf we read the following account of the spirit of this virtue:

> For two days now I have experienced a great desire to be a martyr and to endure all the torments the martyrs suffered.
>
> Jesus, my Lord and Savior, what can I give you in return for all the favors you have first conferred on me? I will take from your hand the cup of your sufferings and call on your name. I vow before your eternal Father and the Holy Spirit, before your most holy Mother and her most chaste spouse, before the angels, apostles and martyrs, before my blessed fathers Saint Ignatius and Saint Francis Xavier — in truth I vow to you, Jesus my Savior, that as far as I have the strength I will never fail to accept the grace of martyrdom, if some day you in your infinite mercy should offer it to me, your most unworthy servant.
>
> I bind myself in this way so that for the rest of my life I will have neither permission nor freedom to refuse opportunities of dying and shedding my blood for you, unless at a particular juncture I should consider it more suitable for your glory to act otherwise at that time. Further, I bind myself to this so that, on receiving the blow of death, I shall accept it from your hands with the fullest delight and joy of spirit. For this reason, my beloved Jesus, and because of the surging joy which moves me, here and now I

---

[268] Cf. ST IIa IIae, q. 123, a. 6.

The Unitive Stage

offer my blood and body and life. May I die only for you, if you will grant me this grace, since you willingly died for me. Let me so live that you may grant me the gift of such a happy death. In this way, my God and Savior, I will take from your hand the cup of your sufferings and call on your name: Jesus, Jesus, Jesus![269]

Prudence

Prudence at this level is exemplified by the perfect acting out of that which is best for our eternal destiny. It is the unique moral virtue that enables us to determine a reasonable milieu between excess and deficiency. Inconsideration, indecision, inconstancy, or rashness is non-existent at this point. At this point we recognize the true good and are able to direct the other virtues to accomplish this good. Prudence at this stage is powerfully engulfed by the Spirit's gift of counsel to such an extent that we inevitably experience a supernatural sense or intuition of what ought to be done or not done. The hunger for truth is the focus of this stage in the experience of the virtue of prudence.[270]

Justice

Immense distress moves us to launch a cry of alarm. Where is love for those who have been refused the right to live? For those who have been killed, mutilated, or imprisoned because they roam the streets? For those who have been exploited at an early age in forced labor or the commerce of perversion? For those whom famine has thrown on the roads of exile? For those who have been made to carry

---

[269] *The Jesuit Relations and Allied Documents* (Cleveland: The Burrow Brothers, 1898), 164, 166.
[270] Cf. ST IIa IIae, q. 47, a. 7.

147

arms? Where is love for those who have been left without a school education and have been condemned to illiteracy? Where is love for those whose family has been destroyed and displaced?[271] *Pope John Paul II*

Justice is the upholding of what is right and fair. In the unitive stage justice takes on the heroic aspect of radically rendering to each person that which he or she is due as a child of God. Theft, fraud, lying, hypocrisy, calumny, slander, derision, simulation, raillery, and so forth, are non-existent in us at this stage and we avoid any aspect of injustice with miraculous fervor.

This fervor, however, is accompanied by the perfect living out of *epikeia*, the spirit of the law. The person who lives the life of heroic justice is a person who, as Evagrius Ponticus describes, "considers himself one with all men because he seems constantly to see himself in every man."[272]

The Heroic Evangelical Counsels

Poverty

It would be a shame for us to be richer than Jesus, who for our sake endured poverty.[273] *Mother Teresa*

"Blessed are you poor, for yours is the kingdom of God" (Lk 5:20). The focus of the mystic at this stage is on living on the bare minimum. Imitation of Christ's poverty is the desire of such a person. The mystic experiences a holy fear for those whose souls are at risk because of comfort and wealth. The contrast between the

---

[271] John Paul II, *Papal Wisdom* (New York: Dutton, 1995), 62.
[272] Evagrius Ponticus, *The 153 Chapters on Prayer*, 125.
[273] Mother Teresa, *Heart of Joy*, 137.

wealthy and the dying poor becomes a source of pain in the mystic. It becomes a sharing in the cross of Jesus Christ.

Chastity

Chastity becomes the great liberating gift of God at this juncture. No longer are the distractions of the flesh a hindrance to the spiritual life. In the married person, chastity enables a person to give his or her being fully, without doubt or reservation, to his or her spouse. Authentic conjugal love at its ecstatic apex takes place at this level of the relationship. For the celibate, freedom becomes the all-encompassing reality of existence. One is free to be fully, without doubt or reservation, a person that is radically for others.

Obedience

> One cannot hide the fact that active life is full of risks because of the numerous opportunities that it offers for sin. But we can be confident of God's special protection in every action we carry out under the sign of obedience.... Doubting when obedience calls you to action is something that deserves the reproach to Peter: "How little faith you have!"[274]
>
> Submit to your superiors, just like ivy. Ivy cannot live if it does not hold fast to something; you will not grow or live in holiness unless you hold fast to obedience.[275]
>
> *Mother Teresa*

Self-centeredness is replaced by other-centeredness. The concern is with doing all that is for the glory and honor of God. There is an abnegation of self-will at this level. This is easily seen

---
[274] Ibid., 97.
[275] Ibid., 83.

in the life of a holy religious. The brother or sister in a religious congregation is obedient to all orders, even the most difficult orders, even the most misguided orders, as long as they do not contradict God's will, honor, and glory. Obedience at this stage is the radical following of Christ's Way. It images the Son's obedience to his Father.

Degrees of the Unitive Life

> The lover asked his Beloved if there was anything remaining in him which was still to be loved. And the Beloved answered that he still had to love that by which his own love could be increased.[276] *Ramon Lull*

In the *passive purification of the spirit* we encounter the experience of *arid mystical union*.[277] In the unitive stage, the mystic progresses to experience an *ecstatic union* with God and for the very few a *transforming union* in God. For the great mystics, the *transforming union*, the highest form of union with God on earth, is attained. These are the *divinized*.

Ecstatic Union

> I am wounded by love. Love urges me to speak of love. Gladly do I give myself up to the service of love…. Do you not feel as if sometimes you were shot through the heart when the fiery dart of this love penetrates the inmost mind of man, pierces his affections so that he can in no way contain or hide the burning of his desire. He burns

---

[276] Ramon Lull, *The Book of the Lover and Beloved*, trans. E. Allison Peers (Mahwah: Paulist Press, 1978), n. 1.

[277] *Interior Castle*, 4th and 5th mansions and chapter 1 of the 6th mansion.

with desire, his affections are stirred, he is in fever and gasps, sighing deeply and drawing long breaths.... Thus, the fever of love, often waning but always returning more acutely, gradually weakens the spirit, wears down and exhausts the strength, until it completely conquers the soul and lays it low.[278]   *Richard of St. Victor*

Ecstasy is the suspension of the exterior senses, the loss of the use of the senses. It is a movement of the entire person's being, body and soul, toward God. It is an experience that may last a few moments, a few minutes, or at times for an entire day or days.[279] A vision at times is the prelude to this experience. But at all times, the person experiencing this ecstasy swoons as he or she becomes ravished and absorbed in the purity of God's love. The body is wounded with the wound of love. Ecstasy ends with an awakening whereby the person slowly recovers the use of the senses.[280]

Rapture

The spiritual experience of rapture is one that is experienced by some, yet it need not be experienced by all who progress toward the *transforming union*.[281] The person who experiences a rapture is a person who senses the very core of his or her being seized by God and carried away into another dimension of reality, a new divine region.[282] This rapture adds something to ecstasy; it adds a certain impulsive, intense, turbulent, jarring, jolting, fervent as-

---

[278] *Richard of Saint Victor: Selected Writings on Contemplation*, trans. Clare Kirchberger (New York: Harper and Brothers, 1957), 213-233.
[279] *Interior Castle*, 6th mansion, Ch. 6.
[280] *Interior Castle*, 6th mansion, Ch. 2; *Life*, Ch. 20, par. 2; *Treatise*, Bk. VII, Ch. 4f.
[281] *Interior Castle*, 6th mansion, Ch. 9.
[282] *Interior Castle*, 6th mansion, Ch. 5.

pect to the experience.[283] It is as if the person's core is inebriated with the overabundance of God. The person's being is overwhelmed by a rushing flood of God's presence. It is not unusual to see the process toward the *spiritual marriage* — which we will take up in the next section — end in rapture.[284]

The Effects of the Ecstatic Union

The primary effect of the *ecstatic union* is the purification of love. By purifying the person's love, the person is prepared to enter in response to grace into the *transforming union*. The mystic at this level has reached the pinnacle of detachment, the pinnacle of sorrow for sin. The person has reached the apex of avoiding all that separates him or her from God. Crosses are no longer feared but embraced as a sharing in the life of the Savior. Suffering becomes a precious gift.[285]

Transforming Union

> Resemblance to God is the whole of man's perfection. To refuse to be perfect is to be at fault.[286]
> *William of St. Thierry*

Once the person has progressed past the *ecstatic union*, the person reaches the summit of the mystical life, the *transforming union*. At this juncture of the mystical life one experiences the ultimate luminous, sweet, and penetrating experience of grace, of God. It is the culmination of the development of the life of grace.[287]

---

[283] ST IIa IIae, q. 175, a. 2 ad ium.
[284] *Interior Castle*, 6th mansion, Ch. 4.
[285] *Life*, Ch. 29; *Dark Night*, Bk. II, Ch. 11f; *Living Flame*, St. 1, v. 2-4; St. 2, v. 1-3.
[286] *William of St. Thierry: The Golden Epistle*, n. 259.
[287] *Living Flame*, St. 2; *Spiritual Canticle*, Part III, St. 22f.

The essential nature of the *transforming union* is marked, as a rule, by the cessation of ecstasies. The person's very being has developed beyond this point in the spiritual journey. One's entire faculties are drawn to the very core of one's being, where the Trinity dwells.[288]

Spiritual Betrothal and Spiritual Marriage

The summit of union on this earthly journey ends in the *spiritual marriage* between a person and his or her Creator. As with every relationship that ends in marriage, there is a time of *betrothal*, a transitory time of union that awaits the *spiritual marriage*, that perfect, continuous union of life and love.[289] In the *spiritual marriage* we become so intimately united with God that we become, as St. John of the Cross so powerfully explains, God by participation:

> The spiritual marriage is incomparably greater than the spiritual betrothal, for it is a total transformation in the Beloved, in which each surrenders the entire possession of self to the other with a certain consummation of the union of love. The soul thereby becomes divine, God through participation, insofar as is possible in this life.... It is accordingly the highest state attainable in this life.[290]

Effects of the Transforming Union

The virtues and the Spirit's gifts have received their full development, as full as is humanly possible on this earthly journey. Sin for all practical purposes is no longer possible, not even venial sins. One has become in a sense deified. One has become God by

---

[288] *Living Flame*, St. 2.
[289] *Spiritual Canticle*, St. 14-15; *Interior Castle*, 7th mansion, Ch. 2.
[290] *Spiritual Canticle*, St. 22, 3.

participation. For William of St. Thierry, "man becomes through grace what God is by nature."[291] And as St. John of the Cross so eloquently puts it,

> [When one has reached the top of the mountain] the soul will be clothed in a new understanding of God in God (through removal of the old understanding) and in a new love of God in God, once the will is stripped of all the old cravings and satisfactions. And God will vest the soul with new knowledge when the other old ideas and images are cast aside (Col 3:9). He causes all that is of the old self, the abilities of one's natural being, to cease, and he attires all the faculties with new supernatural abilities. As a result, one's activities, once human, now become divine.[292]

The Spiritual Senses

> God be in my head and in my understanding. God be in my eyes and in my looking. God be in my mouth and in my speaking. God be in my heart and in my thinking. God be at my end and my departing. *Sarum Primer*

One who has reached the level of the unitive stage experiences reality in a completely different light. One experiences what has often been referred to as the spiritualization of the senses or what is referred to as the *mystical senses*, whereby all of reality is seen differently. "It is no longer I who live" (Gal 2:20). The person is in the sphere of spiritual sensitivity and discernment. A person enters a sphere where he or she has, in a manner, as St. Gregory of Nyssa mentions, "two sets of senses, one corporeal and

---

[291] *William of St. Thierry: The Golden Epistle*, n. 263.
[292] *Ascent*, Bk. I, Chs. 5, 7.

The Unitive Stage

the other spiritual...."[293] As Origen, one of the great ecclesiastical writers of the third century states:

> Since Christ is a "fountain" and "rivers of living water flow from him" (cf. Jn 7:38), and since he is "bread" and gives "life," it should not seem strange that he is also "nard" and "gives forth fragrance" and is the "ointment" (cf. Sg 1:12) by which those who are anointed themselves become Christ, as it says in the Psalm: "Touch not my Christs" (Ps 105:15). And perhaps, according to what the Apostle says, in those "who have their faculties trained by practice to distinguish good from evil" (cf. Heb 5:14), each one of the senses of the soul becomes Christ. For that is why he is called the "true light" (cf. 1 Jn 2:8) so that the souls might have eyes with which to be illumined; and why he is called the "Word" (cf. Jn 1:1), that they might have ears with which to hear; and why he is called "bread of life" (cf. Jn 6:35), that the souls might have a sense of taste with which to taste. So too is he called "ointment" or "nard" so that the soul's sense of smell might receive the fragrance of the Word. And so too is he called perceivable, and touchable by hand, and the "Word became flesh" (cf. Jn 1:14), so that the inner hand of the soul might be able to make contact with the Word of Life.... What do you think they will do when the Word of God takes over their hearing and sight and touch and taste? and when he gives to each of their senses the powers of which they are naturally capable? So that the eye, once able to see "his glory, glory as of the only Son from the Father" (Jn 1:14), no longer wants to see anything else, nor the hearing want to hear anything other than the "Word of life" (1 Jn 1:1)..., nor will the taste,

---

[293] *From Glory to Glory: Texts from Gregory of Nyssa's Mystical Writings*, ed. and intro. Jean Danielou, S.J., trans. and ed. Herbert Musurillo, S.J. (New York: Charles Scribner's Sons, 1961), 156.

once it has "tasted the goodness of the Word of God" (Heb 6:5) and his flesh... (Jn 6:33, 52-58), be willing to taste anything else after this.... For just as in the body there are different senses of tasting and seeing, so are there... divine faculties of perception.[294]

Through the spiritual senses one sees reality through the eyes of God.

In Conclusion

The Christian of the future will either be a mystic or nothing at all. These are the words of the great twentieth century theologian and Jesuit priest Karl Rahner.[295] We are all called to be mystics. To the extent that we respond to God's grace is to the extent that we will enter into the realm where a taste of heaven can be acquired even here on earth, where a taste of perfect happiness, peace and contentment can be found. May we all seek to become saints. May we live the words expressed by the prayer of Karl Rahner:

> Son of the Father, Christ who lives in us, you are our hope of glory. Live in us, bring our life under the laws of your life, make our life like to yours. Live in me, pray in me, suffer in me, more I do not ask. For if I have you I am rich; those who find you have found the power and the victory of their life. Amen.[296]

---

[294] From *Origen, Spirit and Fire: A Thematic Study of His Writings*, by Hans Urs von Balthasar, trans. Robert J. Daly, S.J. (Washington, DC: The Catholic University of America Press, 1984), 220-221.

[295] Rahner, *Theological Investigations*, vol. 7, *Further Theology of the Spiritual Life*, trans. David Bourke (New York: Herder and Herder, 1971), 15.

[296] Rahner, *Everyday Faith*, 210-211.

The Unitive Stage

The apex of the spiritual journey is the living in and with reality — the way one was intended to live in and with it. At the apex of the spiritual journey we become in total harmony with all of creation, for all of creation bears the mark of the one who sustains it. This apex of experience is powerfully reflected in St. Francis of Assisi's *The Canticle of Brother Sun*:

> Most High Almighty Good Lord,
> Yours are the praises, the glory, the honor, and all blessings!
> To You alone, Most High, do they belong.
> And no man is worthy to mention You.
> Be praised, my Lord, with all Your creatures,
> Especially Sir Brother Sun,
> By whom you give us the light of day!
> And he is beautiful and radiant with great splendor.
> Of You, Most High, he is a symbol!
> Be praised, my Lord, for Sister Moon and the Stars!
> In the sky You formed them bright and lovely and fair.
> Be praised, my Lord, for Brother Wind
> And for the Air, cloudy and clear, and all Weather,
> By which you give sustenance to Your creatures!
> Be praised, my Lord, for Sister Water,
> Who is very useful and humble and lovely and chaste!
> Be praised, my Lord, for Brother Fire,
> By whom You give us light at night,
> And he is beautiful and merry and mighty and strong!
> Be praised, my Lord, for our Sister Mother Earth,
> Who sustains and governs us,
> And produces fruits with colorful flowers and leaves!
> Be praised, my Lord, for those who forgive for love of You
> And endure infirmities and tribulations.
> Blessed are those who shall endure them in peace,
> For by You, Most High, they will be crowned!
> Be praised, my Lord, for our Sister Bodily Death,
> From whom no living man can escape!

Woe to those who shall die in mortal sin!
Blessed are those whom she will find in your most holy will,
For the Second Death will not harm them.
Praise and bless my Lord and thank Him
And serve Him with great Humility.[297]

This is the canticle from a man immersed in the love of God, neighbor, and creation. This is a description of a man in love with all of God's reality. This is the image of what we are meant to be. May we seek to live it!

May the Blessed Trinity grant us to arrive at this inmost ground where its true image dwells. Amen.[298]

Johannes Tauler

---

[297] *The Little Flowers of St. Francis*, trans. Raphael Brown (New York: Doubleday, 1958), 317-318.

[298] Johannes Tauler, *Sermons*, trans. Maria Shrady (Mahwah: Paulist Press, 1985), 108.

Appendix

Explaining Salvation and Mysticism in People of Other Faiths

The Anonymous or Implicit Christian

The Christian is called to believe in the triune God who through Christ established his Church, without which no salvation is possible for the world, and in particular or more specifically for the individual. Faith in Christ and faith in his Church are necessary elements for salvation as proclaimed by the Gospel.[299] Scripture (e.g., Mk 16:16; Ac 2:44-47, 12; Heb 11:6; Eph 4:11, 12), the Fathers of the Church (from the time of the Apostolic Fathers, e.g., St. Ignatius of Antioch, to the end of the Patristic age, e.g., St. John Damascene),[300] and the Church Councils (e.g., Trent, Fourth Lateran, etc.)[301] all point out the necessity of Christ and his Church for salvation.

But what about the people who lived before Christ? What about the people who never heard the explicit Gospel message or

---

[299] See Karl Rahner, *Theological Investigations*, vol. 6, *Concerning Vatican II*, trans. Karl and Boniface Kruger (Baltimore: Helicon Press, 1969), 391 for a detailed analysis of this.

[300] William A. Jurgens, ed., *The Faith of the Early Fathers* (Minnesota: The Liturgical Press, 1979), vols. 1-3.

[301] See *The Christian Faith*, ed. Josef Neuner, S.J. and Jacques Dupuis, S.J. (Staten Island: Alba House, 2001).

even heard the word "Christ"? What about those who believe in God yet have not grasped the explicit presentation of the Gospel message? Are all who *through no fault of their own* profess a different belief condemned to hell? What about the person who is swayed by other philosophies? What about the person who seems "turned off" by so-called "Christians"? Reflection and perception warn us that such a profession of condemnation is problematic. How can we condemn such a massive number of people, especially if no sign of subjective guilt can be found in them?[302] If Christ is who Christians claim him to be, then the Christ-event must have meaning in the living experiences of all people, whether they are aware of it or not. Otherwise, Christ would simply be a "nice guy" or solely a good example as opposed to "the Savior."

Karl Rahner's theory of the anonymous Christian or as he later termed it, the implicit Christian, is the key to salvation for others who on the exterior appear to be non-Christians and yet appear to be people of great holiness. These people in fact can be very much great mystics, albeit with great difficulty.

Because of the possibility of an experience of God at the very core of one's innermost being, salvation is a possibility for a vast number of non-Christians who have "through no fault of their own," never heard the explicit expression of Christianity.

Rahner explains that Scripture shows us that God wills all to be saved and reach the summit of truth (1 Tm 2:4). Christ came for all, to save all.

We are faced with two realities when dealing with the Church's infallible teaching. On the one hand the Christian faith as expressed by Christ and his Church is necessary for salvation, and on the other hand, one recognizes that God desires all to be saved. From these two realities one must come to the conclusion that somehow all people are able to become members, in some

---

[302] Rahner, *Theological Investigations*, vol. 6, 391.

sense, of the Church if all are to have the opportunity to be saved. If all people are capable of becoming members of the Church, this implies that there are degrees of becoming members of the Church, degrees of membership. In becoming a Christian one is baptized, accepts the fullness of the faith, and embraces the liturgical life in holiness. Even before the presentation of the explicit Church's preaching of the Gospel message by a missionary effort, one must recognize the movement of grace that allows the person to accept and embrace the message and give it life and light. Likewise, in the case of someone who has never been presented with the Church's preaching, that grace — which is the grace of Christ — is active in the individual and is seeking the fulfillment of its nature to become Christian in all its dimensions even though the preaching of the message may not be present explicitly.[303]

> If it be true that the man who is the object of the Church's missionary endeavor is or can be already prior to it a man who is on the way toward his salvation and finds it in certain circumstances without being reached by the Church's preaching, and if it be true at the same time that the salvation which he achieves is the salvation of Christ, because there is no other, then it must be possible to be not only an anonymous 'theist,' but also an anonymous Christian and this (since the Church of Christ is not a purely interior reality) not in any merely intangible way, but also with a certain making visible and tangible of the anonymous relationship.[304] *Karl Rahner*

---

[303] Rahner, *Theological Investigations*, vol. 6, 391-392. Also cf. CCC 847 citing LG 16: "Those who, through no fault of their own, do not know the Gospel of Christ or his Church, but who nevertheless seek God with a sincere heart, and, moved by grace, try in their actions to do his will as they know it through the dictates of their conscience — those too may achieve eternal salvation."

[304] Rahner, *Theological Investigations*, vol. 6, 392.

Grace is a gratuitous gift of God's self-communicating love to humanity. This grace offered to humanity presupposes an ability to accept and respond to this free gift of love, of presence. The grace presupposes a "being of unlimited openness for the limitless being of God...."[305] It is an openness to a God of mystery who is beyond the limits of all reality, of all that is comprehensible, yet it is an openness to a providential God who is the source and sustainer of all existence, of all reality. The person in his or her whole being has an innate attraction or tendency toward God. This tendency is capable of being open to hearing the absolute, mysterious, often hidden God who transcends all of reality.[306]

Failure to be open to God's gratuitous gift of self leads one to self-contradiction. One inevitably contradicts what one was meant to be. By being radically open, by experiencing transcendence, one is experiencing grace's content. The revelation of the Word, of the Christ, is the expression and explication of what one already is by virtue of grace, by virtue of one's radical openness, one's transcendence.[307] It is a revelation that speaks to a person's being whenever the person completely accepts himself or herself.[308]

When one accepts one's being for what one truly is or was intended to be, one is accepting the reality of Christ as the perfection and guarantee of one's grace-filled movement toward God, a grace-filled movement of the permanent and visible presence of Christ's Body, the Church.[309]

The anonymous or implicit Christian is one who accepts being ordered to God, and who is in harmony — possibly even con-

---

[305] Ibid.
[306] Ibid.
[307] Rahner, *Theological Investigations*, vol. 14, *Ecclesiology, Questions in the Church: The Church in the World*, trans. David Bourke (New York: The Seabury Press, 1976), 394.
[308] Ibid., 395.
[309] Ibid., 394.

fusedly — with his or her own being giving glory to God. From here the person seeks to be actualized, fulfilled, to move from an implicit Christian reality to an explicit Christian reality. Given historical circumstances, the explicitness of the Christian expression may not be able to be actualized without the explicit presentation of Christianity; hence, the person's nature will seek its fulfillment, *in grace*, in an authentically loving and humane spirit. If, however, a higher state of explicitness is offered or presented to the individual, his or her nature will most likely embrace this explicit expression of the faith — an explicit, conscious profession of Church membership. It is in this actualization in God, in grace, that happiness, peace, contentment, and the mystical experience can be found. It is in this mystery — this experience of the triune God — that one finds the fulfillment of what one is intended to be.[310]

For the Christian, salvation and mysticism are inescapably linked to Christ the sanctifier and redeemer. In Christianity, the precondition for salvation and holiness, there is an entrance into the life, death and resurrection of Christ and his body the Church. For the Christian, one's salvation, one's holiness, one's mysticism is *in* Christ, *through* Christ, and *with* Christ.

Therefore, one may argue that the theory of the anonymous Christian or implicit Christian is a plausible way to express the reality of Christ as the *way*, the *truth*, and the *life* in people of other *explicit* faiths. It is one way to express the reality of mysticism outside the sphere of *explicit* Christianity.

---

[310] Ibid.

ST PAULS

This book was produced by St. Pauls/Alba House, the Society of St. Paul, an international religious congregation of priests and brothers dedicated to serving the Church through the communications media.

For information regarding this and associated ministries of the Pauline Family of Congregations, write to the Vocation Director, Society of St. Paul, P.O. Box 189, 9531 Akron-Canfield Road, Canfield, Ohio 44406-0189. Phone (330) 702-0359; or E-mail: spvocationoffice@aol.com or check our internet site, www.albahouse.org